KEEP IT SIMPLE

KEEP IT SIMPLE

A Guide to Assistive Technologies

Ravonne A. Green and Vera Blair

⬤ LIBRARIES UNLIMITED

AN IMPRINT OF ABC-CLIO, LLC
Santa Barbara, California • Denver, Colorado • Oxford, England

Library of Congress Cataloging-in-Publication Data

Green, Ravonne A.
    Keep It Simple : A Guide to Assistive Technologies / Ravonne A. Green and Vera Blair.
      p. cm
    Summary: "This book offers simple, straightforward guidance for the practitioner who wants to use assistive technologies to extend library access" — Provided by publisher.
    Includes bibliographical references and index.
    ISBN 978–1–59158–866–5 (pbk. : acid-free paper) ISBN 978–1–59158–867–2 (e-book)
1. Libraries and people with disabilities. 2. Self-help devices for people with disabilities
3. Libraries and people with visual disabilities. 4. Libraries and the hearing impaired.
I. Blair, Vera. II. Title.
Z711.92.H3G74   2011
027.6′63—dc22   2010051785

ISBN: 978–1–59158–866–5
EISBN: 978–1–59158–867–2

15 14 13 12 11   1 2 3 4 5

This book is also available on the World Wide Web as an eBook.
Visit www.abc-clio.com for details.

Libraries Unlimited
An Imprint of ABC-CLIO, LLC

ABC-CLIO, LLC
130 Cremona Drive, P.O. Box 1911
Santa Barbara, California 93116-1911

This book is printed on acid-free paper ∞

Manufactured in the United States of America

I would like to dedicate this book to my mother, Yvonne Green. My mother read many books to me and instilled in me a love for reading. I would like to dedicate this book to my aunt, Margaret Rogers who taught me to operate audiovisual equipment as a toddler. Now my mother and my Aunt Margaret suffer with macular degeneration and are dependent on assistive technologies and large print. They are both determined to conquer this disability and continue to enjoy reading and listening to books. This book is for all of those we love that can live more productive, useful lives with the help of assistive technology and understanding family members, friends, and colleagues.

Ravonne A. Green

I would like to dedicate this book first to my husband Dr. Wally Koehler who encouraged me to apply to graduate school and get an MLIS degree. Special thanks to Dr. Ravonne Green who suggested collaborating on this book and who did all the footwork of finding a publisher. Thanks to my mother Dorothee, who was nearly blind and deaf at her death and who was a large part of the reason for my early interest in assistive technology. Thanks to my son Heath who was always there to help when the Word Processor tried to get the better of me; and thanks to my children Stephanie and Eric who are always in my heart.

Vera Blair

CONTENTS

PREFACE

ASSISTIVE TECHNOLOGY ISSUES AND GUIDELINES

Green (1999) conducted a national Delphi professional panel consisting of 12 librarians, assistive technology, and disability services experts to determine appropriate guidelines for implementing AT services in academic libraries.[1] This study predicted that if librarians plan AT services and training, and market AT services using a collaborative approach that would include librarians, faculty, staff, and students with disabilities that AT services could be better provided for students with print disabilities. The panel suggested that funding issues should be resolved in some cases by working co-operatively with other departments and community agencies. The panel made the following specific recommendations.

Equipment

The main problems indicated from the above study were: identifying appropriate equipment; incompatibility between AT and library electronic systems such as online public access catalogs (OPAC); screen reading navigation tools for the OPAC; and real time print captioning. Making the OPAC accessible to all users should be a priority item because this would be considered a reasonable accommodation under the ADA.

Funding

Adequate funding for AT, AT personnel, AT training, and funding for AT upgrades were the primary issues in the funding category. The panelists recommended incorporating AT training into other staff trainings and

Table P.1   Important Issues

The following issues were considered by the panelists to be critical or urgent problems or issues. These issues should have first-order priority when planning library AT policies and guidelines.

Equipment
Maintaining equipment
Identifying appropriate equipment
Real-time print text alternative (scans print to screen reader or Braille)
Real time print text enlargement
Accessibility options control panel available on all library computers
Screen reading navigation tools for card catalog
Real time print captioning on video materials
Incompatibility between AT and library electronic systems (i.e., online catalogs)
Training
Finding AT consultants and trainers
Hiring support personnel
Training support personnel
Training librarians to use AT
Identifying AT training needs for students
Providing AT training for students
AT should be user-friendly
AT should be easy to trouble-shoot
Institutional support for AT training
Accessibility
Availability of AT services to students with disabilities
Study table height
Height and location of computer stations
Book and material retrieval services
Access to reserve materials
Help for AT should be accessible
Signage should be easily visible and find-able
AT should be accessible in a non-stigmatizing way
Funding
Adequate funding for AT
Adequate funding for AT personnel

Adequate funding for AT training
Adequate funding for AT upgrades
Marketing
Involve students/faculty/staff with disabilities in AT decisions and marketing AT services
Consumer advisory committee
Campus and library awareness of AT needs and issues
Advertise AT in library handouts
Guidelines
ADA compliance plan
Line item budgeting for AT personnel and services
Collaborative planning with university AT services, Student Disability Services, ADA/AAEEO Offices
Collaborative Agreements between departments
Commitment from library director
Consumer advisor committee with individuals with disabilities
User instruction materials should be accessible in necessary formats for all AT
Mechanism for disseminating policy
Develop library AT guidelines with Disability Resource Center, vendors and others who will be using AT or participating in AT training
Staff sensitivity training
Headphones should be available for AT in open areas
Materials should be available in electronic format
Library databases should be networked with other campus resources

*Items receiving at least two-thirds of the panelists' votes.

assigning staff members partial responsibilities for AT as temporary measures. Gradually, funding should be allocated specifically for AT and disability services training. Funding may be provided by various campus and community agencies.

Training

Inadequate training of AT staff in libraries and inadequate training opportunities for students with disabilities who need to use AT equipment were paramount concerns for members of the Delphi panel. The panel suggested some of the following guidelines for providing training for these individuals: Regularly planned technical and sensitivity training for librarians,

AT training accountability should be built in to staff performance evaluations; collaborative agreements should be made with other institutions to share AT knowledge and resources; and guidelines should be developed co-operatively between vendors, Student Disability Resource Centers, and others participating in AT training. Many training opportunities do not involve cost or can be provided inexpensively.

Accessibility

Providing AT equipment in the most integrated setting possible during regular library hours was a primary concern in the area of accessibility for the panelists. Specifically, the panelists noted insisting on the availability of AT services, accessibility of study tables and AT stations, book and material retrieval services, access to reserve materials, and providing help for patrons in a non-stigmatizing way as being the most important issues. Some of the guidelines suggested by the panelists for providing accessibility included developing an ADA compliance plan, making user instruction materials accessible in necessary formats, and networking library databases with other campus resources.

Marketing

One concern voiced by the experts was that many students are not aware of AT services that are available in the college library or with the process involved with obtaining access to these services. The panelists suggested that campus and library awareness of AT needs and issues should be promoted and that patrons with disabilities should be involved in planning and marketing AT services. The main guideline that the panelists suggested for facilitating marketing AT services was the commitment from the library director to provide AT advertisements, appoint a consumer advisory committee, and plan other AT campus and library awareness strategies.

The findings from the data furnished by the Delphi panel were collected, analyzed, and presented in the following table. Table 1 illustrates the important issues and guidelines that should be included in providing AT services in academic libraries.

In a follow-up study, Green (2008) indicates the same weaknesses as the Green (1999) study.[2] This book will provide guidance for the practitioner for planning accessible library services, selecting appropriate AT, marketing disability services and AT, and training staff in disability services issues and the use of AT. The main focus of the tutorials is Microsoft Windows accessibility and products that are Windows compatible.

Vera Blair contributed the tutorial chapters and web resources at the end of her chapters. Ravonne Green contributed the chapters on accessibility, training, marketing, and universal access. Dr. Green has provided a resource section at the end of each chapter. Both authors welcome your comments and suggestions. Readers may contact the authors at ravonneg@yahoo.com or verablair@yahoo.com.

NOTES

1. Green, Ravonne. *Assistive Technologies for Individuals with Print Disabilities*. Dissertation. Virginia Polytechnic Institute and State University, 1999.

2. Green, Ravonne. "Research Institutions and Library Services for Individuals with Disabilities Survey." 2008. Unpublished survey.

SECTION I
Background

CHAPTER 1

Assistive Technology Background

ASSISTIVE TECHNOLOGY: A DEFINITION

According to the Assistive Technology Act of 2004, assistive technology (AT) (also called *adaptive technology*) refers to any "product, device, or equipment, whether acquired commercially, modified or customized, that is used to maintain, increase, or improve the functional capabilities of individuals with disabilities."[1] Common computer-related assistive technology products include screen magnifiers, large-key keyboards, alternative input devices such as touch screen displays, oversized trackballs and joysticks, speech recognition programs, and text readers.

Most AT are people-related such as information and referral assistance, student training, equipment exchange programs, AT guides and materials, and peer support programs.

Educators have long held to the belief that the college (academic) library is the heart of the institution. Library resources should be accessible to everyone if in fact the library is to be the heart of the institution. Academic library administrators should know the AT that are available, their strengths and weaknesses, and how best to match the AT to the needs of the user. Library administrators should be aware of litigation involving access and accommodations, and funding and training issues to serve students with disabilities effectively.

Definitions of disability will vary somewhat depending on the groups of people surveyed and their own interpretation of the severity of their disability. A sensory disability is defined as blindness or deafness or a serious vision or hearing handicap. A physical disability is defined as a problem with any physical activity like walking. Mental disabilities are defined as cognitive disabilities like learning.

At least one of the six types of disability was reported by 36.1 million people, or 12.1 percent of the civilized non-institutionalized population, in the 2008 American Community Survey (ACS). It is important to note that the 2008 ACS survey altered the question about employability for individuals with disabilities between ages 15 and 65. This change probably accounted for a lower number of individuals reporting disabilities in the 15–65 age group and a decrease in the total percentage of persons with disabilities.[2] More than 50 percent of the population over age 65 have some sort of disability. 13.1 million people depend on some kind of AT device.[3]

Age-related macular degeneration, hearing loss, mobility problems like arthritis and memory loss account for one-third of the disabilities for people over 65. As people age, their relatively mild impairments are likely to become more severe and different disabilities may emerge. Those people who were born with a disability are more likely to have received help in childhood but many older people do not seek help because they do not consider themselves to have a disability.

The Forrester Research Study in 2008 reported that 14.8 million people aged 5 years and older (5.3%) had either a hearing or a vision difficulty.[4] Cognitive disabilities account for about 4.2 percent with most of these being caused by dyslexia or attention-deficit disorder. Speech impairments account for 4 percent of the general population. In real numbers, this represents 45.9 million people who will need visual assistance, 43.7 million will need assistance with dexterity problems, 36.3 million for hearing problems, 33.5 million by cognitive problems, and 6.2 million by speech problems.[5]

Among computer users, about 25 percent have been reported as having difficulty with vision, 24 percent have mobility impairments, and 29 percent of computer users have problems with hearing. Thirty-three million people will need visual aids, 31.2 million will need dexterity aids, 26.5 million will need hearing aids, 21.2 million will need aids for cognitive disabilities, and 3.6 million will need aids for speech disabilities.[6]

The trend toward assistive technologies (AT) and the development of universal access like the built-in computer package by Microsoft and others is a positive step in addressing the need for AT. There are many tools available to individuals with disabilities that are free or inexpensive. We will discuss these by disability type in subsequent chapters. There are computer systems being developed for disability-specific uses and special computer packages for seniors that have all the software installed and are ready to be used when they come from the factory.

Despite the availability of assistive tools, many individuals are not aware of them and have not been trained to use assistive technologies. We would like to foster an awareness of these technologies and to provide tutorial assistance in using some of the more common tools.

This book will provide guidance for the practitioner for planning accessible services, selecting appropriate AT, marketing disability services and AT, and training staff in disability services issues and the use of AT. We will include a tutorial section on available technologies for People with Disabilities. The main focus will be technology applications commonly available on Microsoft Office and other low-cost technologies. The book will provide a resource section for specific disabilities at the end of each chapter. In addition to serving as a guide for practitioners, this book should serve as an aid for individuals with disabilities that are making independent decisions about technologies for themselves.

Libraries in particular must be careful to purchase equipment that is user-friendly and to maintain that equipment and provide technical support to users. People with special needs should be made aware that assistive technology is available in the library.

ASSISTIVE TECHNOLOGY: A HISTORY

The abacus, an ancient Chinese counting device still in use today in many parts of the world, is probably the first mechanical device for individuals with vision impairments. The typewriter, invented by Pellegrini in 1808, is one of the most important assistive technologies.

In the 1800s, an increasingly consistent attempt was made to aid those with disabilities in the form of services to the disabled.[7] In 1817, the Gallaudet school for the hearing impaired was opened by Thomas Hopkins Gallaudet. A few years later, Louis Braille adapted Charles Barbier's "Ecriture Nocturne" or literally translated as (night writing) specifically for Napoleon's army so that he could send military messages to be read in the dark. There were several other codes for the blind invented around the same time, some of them with raised Roman letters but Braille's version would remain the most popular.

In 1872, Alexander Graham Bell began to conduct classes for teachers of the deaf, and in 1876, he invented the telephone, a by-product of his work with individuals with hearing impairments. In 1916, through Harvey Fletcher and Irving Crandal's work at Bell Laboratories on assistive hearing and speech, the electronic hearing aid was developed. Bell Laboratories developed much of the electronic work that led to advances in AT. Until 1940, carbon hearing aids with large batteries were in use, but they were not powerful enough for severe hearing loss. Better quality vacuum tube hearing aids appeared in the 1930s.

In 1921, the amplifier, loudspeaker, and microphone were invented and helped develop the first public address system. The public address system aided the cause for assistive technology because these component parts were developed for people with hearing problems. Analog and digital hearing aids have become smaller since 1986. Hearing aids then led to cochlear implants.[8]

The first reading machine, called the Optophon, was invented in 1920 for the blind by Edmund Fournier D'Albe, a physics lecturer from Birmingham, England. It worked on the principle of converting the shapes of letters into musical sounds heard in a telephone receiver that required a long learning curve for the user. The original price in 1922 was $600 for the Optophon.

The Readphon, invented in 1934, stored literature and music on LPs, a great advance for helping the vision impaired. 1936 marks the year of the artificial speech synthesizer, a development by H.W. Dudley for Bell Laboratories. This technology was another great stride toward assisting individuals with disabilities. In 1948, the first talking book in the form of a tape recording was created. From 1948 on, much time and energy was spent into miniaturizing all the components to aid individuals with hearing and visual impairments. John Bardeed, William Shockley, and Walter Brattain invented the transistor, an important invention toward miniaturization, for Bell Laboratories in 1956 and earned the Nobel Prize for physics.

In 1952, a speech recognition system was developed by Bell Laboratories. In 1964, the TDD (telecommunications device for the deaf) and TTY (teletype) were invented. TDD was at one time the commonly accepted terminology. The TTY is a typewriter that connects to a visual screen, allowing individuals with deafness to communicate with hearing persons. In 1972, the first large-scale packet network was developed that popularized text messaging. This was the ARPAnet, precursor of the Internet, for which the Defense Department was largely responsible.

Kurzweil technology arrived in 1975 with flatbed scanners and the first optical character recognition technology (OCR). OCR allows translation of written text into digital language. The digital language can be translated into audio output or print, including Braille. The Kurzweil 1000 software enables visually impaired or blind persons to read information originally in print or electronic form. The equipment reads text aloud and the voices can be adjusted for personal preference. OCR devices access online materials that may be sent on to Braille embossers or to MP3 and DAISY. Captioning opened new doors for the deaf and hard of hearing in 1960. Captioning facilitated the learning of languages, made foreign films accessible to everyone, and allowed searching video databases by key words.

The Kurzweil 3000 for Windows was first introduced in 1996. Kurzweil 3000 software is helpful for people with cognitive impairments like dyslexia, and can be accessed by alternative means via computer. Kurzweil reads aloud and the user can type directly on to the scanned text.

POPULAR ASSISTIVE TECHNOLOGIES
AVAILABLE FOR LIBRARIES

The simplest and most obvious asset for a library should be a comprehensive selection of large print books, talking books, DAISY formatted books, and Braille books. Closed circuit TVs (CCTVs) that magnify print or stand-alone machines that read print aloud like the POET or SARA are ideal for people with limited technical ability.

Since the mid-1990s, there has been an accelerated increase of technology for individuals with disabilities for personal use. Some of these technologies include voice-activated technology for light switches, TTY telephones, talking caller IDs for the blind, large keypads for telephones, pagers, calculators, and volume control for telephones and talking medical devices like glucose monitors.

Many technology companies produce products that overlap in function. Price ranges are from a few dollars to thousands of dollars. One of the best, simplest, and least expensive pieces of AT for use in libraries or the home today is screen-enlarging software. The ZoomText 9.18 magnifier or magnifier-reader is one of these, but there are many different companies that make similar products. ZoomText 9.18 is compatible with the new Windows 7 operating system and is also 64 bit compatible. Information for ZoomText may be requested at this toll-free number: 866–206–7249. Screen enlarging software is easy to use, there is usually tech support available, and web sites are upgraded regularly. Microsoft offers a variety of assistive technologies in its Windows XP, Vista, and Windows 7 programs—magnification, limited screen reader, volume control, various color and contrast schemes, mouse and cursor settings, and speech processor. These do not have the range that for-cost software programs do but they are free and useful to people with mild to moderate disabilities.

The Kurzweil 3000 reader version 12 (www.kurzweiledu.com) has been a tremendous aid for individuals with visual impairments and learning disabilities. The Kurzweil scans the material, including graphics, into the computer and reads it aloud to the user. This device allows on-screen highlighting of text, annotation, and outlining, as well as separating the outline from the text. Interaction with text rather than passive reading has proven helpful in learning. Kurzweil contains aids such as a dictionary in different languages, and a thesaurus.

The Kurzweil 3000 has word prediction, spellchecking, and bookmarking capabilities. The software requires at least a Pentium or AMD 400 MHz, 128 MB of memory, 2 MB video RAM, sound card with speakers, and a scanner.

Kurzweil 1000 (www.kurzweiledu.com/kurz1000.aspx) is a text-to-speech screen reader for people with visual impairments. It has a choice of different voices, spell check, and e-mail options. Kurzweil 1000 is also available in different languages and it has Braille embossing capability. Kurzweil software automatically installs from a CD. More information is obtainable from the following: customerservice@cambiumlearning.com. Phone number is 800–547–6747, 781–276–0600.

Alternative Input Technology

Examples of specific pieces of alternative input technologies in libraries are:

SmartCat from Cirque software (www.cirque.com/) is a touchpad controller. The user may scroll and zoom with a single touch. It has a unique sound for each operation, combining mouse and touchpad functions in one unit. Trackballs are also commonly available.

SARA (www.freedomscientific.com/products), the scanning and reading appliance with OCR, is another simple unit that reads aloud. SARA connects to a monitor for viewing enlarged print. SARA is compatible with DAISY formatted talking books. It is easy to use without special training and reads many languages. SARA is a newer reader from Freedom Scientific that reads many different file types and identifies currency. The user may select various custom color combinations for the background for easier reading.

MAGic for Windows (www.fredeomscientific.com) is a screen magnifying software for the web from Freedom Scientific. The letters can be magnified to such a degree (up to 36 times) that there are large empty spaces on the screen making it sometimes difficult to track text. The most recent upgrade of this unit is the 11 version, a screen magnifier that either stands alone or has speech support. It is compatible with JAWS and has Braille support.

The MAGic with speech version will read screen contents aloud. The size of the window and the border colors and contrast are adjustable. MAGic tracks with mouse, cursor, tool, or window. This magnifier may be combined with the JAWS unit reader for Windows. It is compatible with Windows 7, Vista (the Home Premium versions), and Windows Server 2008 both with 32 and 64 bit.

JAWS 11 (Job Access With Speech) for Windows from Freedom Scientific (http://www.freedomscientific.com/fs_products/software_jaws.asp) is a screen reader with additional features like Braille compatibility. JAWS allows access to Internet Explorer with links lists, frames lists, HTML tables, and graphics. It allows the user change the sound to point out quotes or boldface text. JAWS is compatible with Windows 7, Vista, Windows 2000, XP, ME, 98, and 95. Sixty megabytes of hard drive-disk space are required as well as a sound card. JAWS works with a variety of commercial word processing tools.

OpenBook version 8, updated November 2008 (http://www .freedomscientific.com/downloads/openbook/openbook-whats-new.asp), is a screen-reading and scanning software. It works with Windows 7, Vista, XP, and Windows 2000.

Window-Eyes 7 from GW Micro (http://www.gwmicro.com/Window -Eyes/) is a screen reader for those with visual impairments allowing instant access to Windows-based systems. This version has added Braille capability.

Refreshable Braille units, Braille printers, as well as TTY should be available in a library.

Another impressive piece of software is *Dragon Naturally Speaking*, a speech recognition system. Dragon works with Microsoft Word and other systems to write documents from dictation. The software trains with the user's voice. It is compatible with e-mail programs Microsoft Outlook and Microsoft Express, and can be used for web browsing, and replying to e-mail messages. Specialized medical and legal systems of Dragon are available. The advent of digital technology has made it possible to translate among vision, sound, and tactile languages.

ASSISTIVE TECHNOLOGY PRODUCTS

The Microsoft web site offers complete descriptions of the following assistive technology products.

Alternative input devices
Braille embossers
Keyboard filters
Light signaler alerts
On-screen keyboards
Reading tools and learning disabilities programs
Refreshable Braille displays
Screen enlargers, or screen magnifiers
Screen readers
Speech recognition or voice recognition programs
Text-to-Speech (TTS) or speech synthesizers
Talking and large-print word processors
TTY/TDD conversion modems

STEPS TO EVALUATE ASSISTIVE TECHNOLOGY SOLUTIONS

The Assistive Technology Decision Tree is an excellent tool for determining an appropriate fit for assistive technology and individual needs. The assistive technology tree will help your organization and an individual with disabilities to define the problem and to answer questions about modifying the work environment, finding appropriate assistive technologies, and finding other potentially satisfactory solutions. This tool may be found at http:// docs.google.com/viewer.

ACCESSIBILITY ISSUES

W3C, the Worldwide Web Consortium, offered the WAI or Web Accessibility Initiative in 1997. W3C takes into consideration all types of disabilities—visual, hearing, cognitive, and physically challenged in any way. There are organizations that specialize in making web pages universally accessible. DO-IT (Disabilities, Opportunities, Internetworking, and Technology at the University of Washington) provides a list of Internet resources at http://weber.u.washington.edu/~doit/. BOBBY, the accessibility program, is no longer free or stand-alone. It is now part of an IBM software package.

There are other issues to consider when discussing access to library materials for individuals with disabilities. Physical access issues involve getting to the library and physically accessing the collection. The following questions should be kept in mind when considering physical access. Is there a bus or pick-up service? Is there wheelchair accommodation? Have staff been trained to work with individuals with disabilities? Is technical help available for assistive software? Are workstations adjustable (at least 30 inches high to accommodate wheelchairs)? Often rooms for individuals with disabilities in libraries are away from the mainstream and difficult to access. Many older people are not comfortable enough using technology and are not able to use it without some help. The educational level and age of people using the library must be considered when choosing assistive technology aids. A public library would need simpler technology than an academic library.

A person's disability may be an inability to enter information into a computer due to paralysis or coordination problems that prevent the use of a mouse or keyboard. For these people, alternate input devices must be used, such as voice-command or rocker switches. There are micro keyboards for patrons with limited mobility, large-key keyboards for people with coordination problems, and trackball or touchpad controllers, touchpads, and on-screen keyboards to allow people with limited manual dexterity to provide input into a computer. People who need assistance in getting information from the computer may also need assistive devices. For example, screen magnifiers, Braille readers, large print screen, text to Braille, and Braille to audio translators, refreshable Braille (screens that allow a person to feel Braille letters on a mouse or computer screen) may be needed.

New technologies like DAISY allow talking books to be navigated, making them more useful for individuals with disabilities. DAISY ("Digital Accessible Information SYstem") is a system of marked-up text linked with audio that allows a person with disabilities to search (an encyclopedia, for instance) more effectively than a straight talking book requiring linear access.

There are general groups of people with disabilities that must be considered when designing rooms with assistive technologies in libraries. Some of these categories might include: those with print-disabilities, such as low vision, blind, or deaf and blind; those with cognitive impairments such as dyslexia and/or poor verbal skills; those with hearing impairments; those with physical impairments such as neuromuscular or skeletal disorders or limited mobility; and those with age-related disabilities, which may include comorbid disabilities.

More and more materials that were formerly available in print format from the government, service organizations, and vendors are now available only on web sites. Older, non-computer literate people have no access to many of these resources.[9] Medical information from drug companies, insurance information, and health information from governmental and local agencies are some of the primary sources of information that older individuals need to access that may not be available in alternative formats. Older people can and do use computers successfully. Senior citizens are the largest population of AT users and libraries should market AT services to this group.

Funding for assistive technology remains a problem. Medicare, Medicaid, and Social Security will cover only some of the costs. Many companies are now investigating a universal design concept, which would make all products more easily accessible by all people. Some design concepts are already being used in the form of the handicapped sign in the computer control panel where some hearing, vision, and motility problems are addressed and alternative keyboard, sound, display, and mouse options are offered. The universal design concept is a product of the Archimedes Project started in 1990, a group of people dedicated to making information accessible to all. The developmental trends are toward wireless systems in libraries that will allow people to bring their own adaptive technology tools. Windows XP, Windows Vista, and Windows 7 are phenomenal pieces of software with assisting devices for visual contrast, audio, speech, mobility, and cognitive disabilities. Librarians can help seniors with disabilities learn what information is available online and demonstrate that those with low vision or hearing loss can access computers with assistive and adaptive technology. Some of the simplest adaptations for libraries that benefit seniors are large monitors, good lighting, adjustable desks and chairs, large computer keys, trackball mice for stiff joints, CCTVs, and magnification software. Microsoft has an Aging and Accessibility web site that covers some of its built-in features like stickykeys, which allows one keystroke for double keystrokes, filterkeys that ignore repeated keystrokes due to tremors, and contrast control.

Staff should receive training in how to approach individuals with disabilities and request information on what assistive devices they need. An advisory committee from a cross section of people with impairments should ensure that all groups are fairly represented. There should be ongoing awareness training for the library staff and information should be sent to the community in large print for easier reading.

More than ever, people with disabilities are seeking higher education and employment. This increase in the last 10 years has been partly due to advances in technology that allow individuals with disabilities to have access to the same information as others.[10] Many individuals with disabilities are now mainstreamed into classrooms. There are support programs, increased public awareness, library access, funding, and continuing research. Adaptive technology is being advanced through faculty and library in-service, technology training sessions, publications, and general marketing. Equipment costs are more affordable.

Access to information fosters self-reliance in individuals with disabilities and they are able to develop to their full potential. Life becomes more manageable with appropriate technologies. Another positive result of information access is to reduce the isolation barriers that previously kept individuals with disabilities at home or in institutions. It provides people with the necessary tools to acquire skills that will help them become independent in a career; it provides basic skills for those with disabilities to build additional skills for self-satisfaction and fun as well as work. This endeavor is truly the dream come true of librarians in providing skills for lifelong learning.

A SIMPLE ASSISTIVE TECHNOLOGY ROOM LAYOUT

The assistive technology room should be large enough to contain two workstations with wheelchair access. Large signs should identify the room as assistive and provide directions to the room. Desks need to be adjustable and monitors need to be on movable arms. Two or more up-to-date computers with Windows XP and Vista and large, 24-inch flat-screen monitors with stand-alone magnifiers like POET or SARA for those with limited computer skills would be must-have items for the AT lab. Alternative input devices, such as a trackball mouse and a joystick, should be included. One very large keyboard with Braille signage should be available; one refreshable Braille unit for one computer to allow blind persons to surf the web, one very small keyboard, as well as a large-format laser printer and Braille printer. Portable Braille printers are available that plug into a USB port. Headphones should be available. One TTY device should be available for hearing challenged persons to communicate with library personnel. The Kurzweil 1000 for blind users and the Kurzweil 3000 (an interactive screen reader that reads aloud and underlines) for developmentally challenged persons would also be useful. The Kurzweil can be used as a web-tool that allows reading aloud from the web. A CCTV is probably the simplest magnifier available. Software like MAGic and JAWS magnifiers with speech capability and web browsing work well but are not user-friendly and require tutoring. Dragon Naturally Speaking is a must for those who cannot type due to mobility problems or because they have never learned. If a whole room is not available, at least a private workstation should be available.

The thing to keep in mind when developing assistive technology for a library is that most of the people who require assistance are not totally blind, deaf, or paralyzed. Many of the users will be older people who have lost some of their vision, hearing, and mobility. Regular courses offered at a library to maximize the use of Windows free technology would be a big step in helping those with minimal assistive needs.

The equipment for a basic AT room can be acquired for around $10,000. This would be a wise investment in the community and would bring many older patrons into the library as well as others with disabilities. Librarians should carefully research what products would make the most sense for their library. Ask patrons with disabilities what they need and include them in the decision-making process. For librarians, whose ethical and moral commitment it is to be a service to the community in promoting lifelong learning for all, it is imperative that they become part of the planning and implementing of assistive technology and disability services.

ACCESSIBILITY OPTIONS ON WINDOWS XP

Many assistive options such as screen magnifiers and screen readers are already built into Windows XP and Vista at no extra cost. We will assume that the PC user will have a Microsoft Office program installed. (There is a new free download available for Microsoft Office 7 and newer versions that allow conversion of documents into DAISY format.) There are options to customize screen display and readability such as color options for more or less contrast, adjusting screen resolution and icon size; and the blink rate of the cursor can be changed or removed altogether. Sound volume can be enhanced; text-to-speech option is available; there are visual alternatives to sounds; and the user can obtain either visual cues or sound cues, whichever are needed. See www.enable.com.

The easiest way to access assistive technology options is by going through the accessibility Wizard. The Wizard prompts the user to select vision, hearing, or other difficulties, and will suggest various options. This is a good start, but the user may want more options, and then it is best to access the individual assistive modules like Mouse, Keyboard, or Speech that offer more options.

Keyboard and Mouse Options

Choose the speed at which to click the mouse; click and drag without holding down the mouse button; change the size, shape, and color of the pointer; and track the pointer on the screen. Reversal of function of the right and left mouse buttons may be set. A great feature for those with limited physical mobility is stickykeys that allows the pressing of keys in turn, rather than together (like alt-cont-del). Togglekeys make tones when depressed and filterkeys set the speed with which the computer accepts depressed keys, ignoring shaky hands or fingers. The pointer may be manipulated by using a joystick or numerical keypad.

Other great options already built-in are a separate window on part of the screen where the pointer is that magnifies letters to an extremely large degree. A voice reads what is on the screen. The rate of the voice reader may be changed to read faster or more slowly, but it remains a computer-generated type sound, very mechanical. This is one option where purchasing a high-quality voice system is worth the investment.

An on-screen keyboard is a built-in option so that users can employ alternative input like joystick, mouthstick, or head tracking device. Care must be exercised when choosing a joystick, because most of them are configured for games, not for computer use and may not work with an on-screen keyboard. An administrative option turns the accessibility options on or off.

THE FUTURE OF TECHNOLOGY

Futurist and inventor Ray Kurzweil, developer of flatbed scanner technology and a speech recognition expert, believes that we are at the edge of an entirely new way of experiencing the world and its progress. Humans and machines, especially artificial intelligence, are combining in new ways to create something larger than either human or machine, and Kurzweil calls this the "Singularity" where progress is no longer linear but has become unpredictable. Humans are in an exponential cultural and technological evolution with human intelligence augmented by human-invented machines.[11]

Many scientists and thinkers speculate that this is the last generation of totally "human" beings, that the next generation will be part machine, with ever-increasing mechanical components, and with consciousness interacting directly with machines.

New inventions are on the horizon that may eventually enable congenitally blind people to see. Scientists have known for some time that stimulating nerve cells in the vision system can enable blind people to have some limited vision experience. A new approach uses a digital camera to feed information into the brain. Visual information from a digital camera is channeled through a signal processor that translates the information into neural impulses and directs them into the visual cortex of the brain.[12]

According to a report by the BBC, Japanese researchers have created the first artificial eyeball. The work was done on frogs using tadpole embryonic cells but scientists hope that some day a similar process may be used on humans.[13]

Scientists have been experimenting with artificial retinas to restore vision. A multiple-unit artificial retina (MARC) chipset is implanted into the eye. This would enable many people, especially the elderly population with retinal degeneration, to see again. A digital camera captures the image and translates it into an electrical signal that is passed on to the remaining intact retinal cells and produces an image that the patient can see.[14]

Scientists at Northwestern University have discovered that it is possible to grow nerve cells on a three-dimensional nanotechnology framework. A three-dimensional nanotechnology framework may enable people with spinal cord and other nerve injuries to regain use of their limbs.[15] From space technology comes artificial rods and cones, the sensors that are responsible for vision in the retina of the eye that convert light signals to electrical signals for processing by the brain. This news comes from the Space Vacuum Epitaxy Center (SVEC) in Houston. Ceramic films, which are light sensitive much like rods and cones, are inserted into the eye to perform the function of natural rods and cones.[16] These technological marvels are not just wishful thinking; they are already in the developmental stages toward practical applications for assistive and adaptive devices, promising a more comfortable and productive living for everyone.

RESOURCES

Key Foundation—http://www.key.org
DAISY Player—http://en.wikipedia.org/wiki/Daisyplayer
Kurzweil Reader—www.kurzweiledu.com/products_k1000.asp
Jaws—www.freedomscientific.com/fs_products/software_jaws
Web Accessibility—http://booboo.webct.com/otln/webct_accessibility.htm
Accessibility—www.ipsoft.co.uk/site/accessibility

NOTES

1. Assistive Technology Act. 2004. *U.S.C.* Vol. 29, sec. 3001.
2. Brault, Matthew. "Review of Changes to the Measurement of Disability in the 2008 American Community Survey," U.S. Census Bureau, September 22, 2009. http://www.census.gov/hhes/www/disability/2008ACS_disability.pdf.
3. Ibid.
4. Forrester Research, Inc., *Findings about Working Age Adults*, 2003, Updated February 14, 2008. http://www.micrsoft.com (April 6, 2009).
5. Forrester Research, Inc., *The Market for Accessible Technology—The Wide Range of Abilities and Its Impact Computer Use*, 2003. http://www. microsoft.com (April 6, 2009).
6. Bryant, Diane Pedroddy and R. Bryant, Brian. *Assistive Technology for People with Disabilities* (Boston: Allyn and Bacon, 2003), pp. 10–11.
7. Mudry, Albert and Dodele, Leon. "History of the Technological development of Air Conduction Hearing Aids," *The Journal of Laryngology & Otology* 114 (2000), pp. 418–423.
8. Mates, Barbara T. "Computer Technology to Aid Special Audiences," in *Library Technology Reports* (ALA: May/June 2006), p. 11. http://www.ala.org/Template.cfm ?Section=archive&template=conten.
9. Prentice, M. "Serving Students with Disabilities at a Community College," (2002), ERIC Digest, (22 August 2005) quoted by Sherry E. Gelbwasser, "Adaptive Technology:

Not Just for People with Disabilities." http://webjunction.org/do/DisplayContent ?id=12114.

10. Mates.

11. Kurzweil, Ray. "The Third Culture," *The Singularity: A Talk with Ray Kurzweil*, 2002, www.edge.org (April 6, 2009).

12. Rowe, Duncan Graham. "Re: Brain Implants to Restore Vision," www.telebio .com/vision (April 8, 2009).

13. Scanlon, Charles. BBC News, "Scientists Create First Artificial Eyeball," January 5, 2002. http://www.bbc.co.uk/2/hi/science/nature/1743987 (accessed April 6, 2009).

14. Humayun, Liu W. M. S. "Electronic-Enhanced Optics, Optical Sensing in Semiconductor Manufacturing, Electro-Optics in Space, Broadband Optical Networks," 2000, in *Digest of the LEOS Summer Topical Meetings*, 2000. 161–162. 101109/LEOSST .2008.869699.

15. Swain, Erik. "Nanostructures a Key to Curing Some Paralyses?" R&D Digest, Originally Published in MDDI March 2004. Devicelink.com/mddiarchive/04/03/016 (April 6, 2009).

16. Science @ NASA, *Bionic Eyes*, http://science.nasa.gov/headlines/y2002/03jan _bioniceyes.htm, January 2003 (accessed April 13, 2009).

SECTION II
Equipment

CHAPTER 2

Print Disabilities

When we think of someone with a print disability, the first thing that comes to mind is the difficulty or inability to read books or newspapers. In the academic world, however, there are many more issues to consider: web page access, electronic access to online catalogs, electronic encyclopedias, dictionaries and other references, and online courses and the databases required to make use of these courses. There are now legal requirements as well as social and ethical considerations to provide access online for those with print disabilities: the information age is here and everyone has a right to equal access of information. As a bonus, some of the devices that enable people with disabilities to function better often are more convenient for everyone, like digital readers for people to listen to while driving.

Print disabilities include blindness as well as difficulties seeing and handling printed material. They include color blindness, age-related macular degeneration, dyslexia and other learning disabilities, concentration difficulties, and age-related mobility problems and paralysis. The inability to hold a book and turn pages is considered a print disability. It is estimated that 10–20 percent of the population has some kind of print disability.[1]

Thinking globally, it is estimated by the World Health Organization that 161 million people have visual impairments. One hundred and twenty-four million of these have reduced vision and 37 million were estimated to be totally blind. Digital services will aid many of these people to enter the information age.[2] This book will discuss print disabilities that involve vision. The concept of print disabilities becomes alarming when considering that only 5 percent of global print material is available in formats accessible to those with print disabilities.[3]

People with disabilities visit the Internet less frequently than do people with no disabilities. Nearly 17 percent of people who use computers report a mild visual disability while 9 percent of computer users report a more challenging visual disability.[4] People with print disabilities rely on information provided in alternative formats: Braille-tactile and print-Braille, DAISY formatted materials, audio, e-text information, and video with descriptions and different languages.

More information is digitized and available from libraries geographically distant, but that is only part of the solution. Even digital information is not readily available to the user if he or she needs equipment other than a computer to access it, like speech synthesizers, Braille readers, or magnifiers.[5] Some or all of these formats are now available in most community libraries and certainly in academic libraries. The revolution in text alternative format has resulted in an accelerated need for librarians and end users to become familiar with the new equipment. When a piece of electronic equipment fails, the library must repair or replace it. Most libraries do not plan for these additional investments in money and time. The inconvenience to patrons and staff when equipment is down is another major concern.

Copyright laws are still not friendly to users of alternative formats. Canada allows persons with a print disability to make or have made alternative format materials with the exception of large print. In Great Britain, copyright law excludes people with learning disabilities from making free alternative copies. Copyright laws should be amended so that they do not prevent persons with a print disability from accessing copyrighted materials through alternative formats. All materials should be made available through the "fair use" clause. PGP, OpenSSL, or GNUPG encryption formats are solutions because they do not hinder accessibility.

Libraries must not only accommodate patrons by providing alternative formats to print materials, but those with print disabilities must learn to use the new materials efficiently.[6] Interlibrary cooperation, collaboration, and sharing of resources is a necessary step in providing alternate format materials like print magnifiers, screen readers, audio books, Braille, and tactile formats to people with print disabilities. Libraries must make an effort to advertise services and products to reach the greatest number of those who need assistive technology.

We have seen an increase in recent years in the type of physical and electronic materials and media available for those with print disabilities. Braille systems are now available in refreshable Braille, which shows the information on the computer with a tactile display of raised pins. Refreshable Braille is especially convenient for libraries because it is silent. Refreshable Braille is an expensive technology. Library staff should be aware of the existence of such materials and make an effort to acquire some of the basic hardware and software for those patrons with vision disabilities. There is a resurgence of interest in the Moon alphabet, a tactile alphabet that is easier to learn than Braille, especially for older people who have lost their vision. Libraries should consider acquiring some equipment in this format.

Digital Talking Books, also known as DAISY, enables people with print disabilities to access and navigate text materials. The DAISY Consortium, formed in 1996, is primarily responsible for the formation of a new international standard for books and information in electronic format. DAISY standards require that information be scannable, readable, and underlinable. In May of 2008, the DAISY Consortium made available its newest DAISY Pipeline, a free download that transforms various different file formats into multimedia formats that are accessible by people with print disabilities (www.daisy.org/projects/pipeline/). The content of DTBs is defined by specifications from NISO Digital Talking Book Standard ANSI/NISO Z39.86. DTBs may contain content ranging from XML text only to text plus audio. This system requires the user to buy and maintain the reasonably priced hardware reader and the library will furnish the DTBs.[7]

Optical Character Recognition (OCR) is another system that has made great strides in recent years. A camera with appropriate software scans the written material and converts it into digital material that reads aloud using a synthesizer. The user may save and translate text into multiple languages or other formats. Newer voices sound more pleasant and less robotic than earlier voices.

New WCAG 2 guidelines address the needs of people with disabilities by taking into consideration all possible disabilities and combinations of disabilities—vision, hearing, speech, mobility, cognitive, and learning disabilities. It addresses perceivability like text alternatives or captions, understandability, and operability. It is easily navigable and accessible with a keyboard.[8]

It is simple to make web content available to those with disabilities by altering format: for instance, by substituting text for images and adding captioned material; or making web content accessible with alternative input. Alternative keyboards including Braille format and digital web content or content that is accessible using assistive technologies are other options.

In a follow-up study of earlier work by Axel Schmetzke where 56 ALA accredited library school web sites were examined for web accessibility, it was discovered that still only 50–60 percent of these web sites were free of errors and fully compliant with WC3 standards. The Bobby program was used to check these web sites. Canadian web sites fared better than U.S. web sites in accessibility. U.S. web sites did not steadily improve between 2002 and 2006.[9]

Even worse, a study of Australian web sites from 2007 indicated that there was no improvement and a slight worsening of accessibility of university web sites with 100 percent of the web sites and 92 percent of individual pages being accessible with mostly text alternatives lacking. Forty-one university web sites were sampled. The tools were HERA, the web Accessibility Toolbar, and the Wave.[10]

CHECKING WEB PAGES FOR WC3 COMPLIANCE

Web pages must be checked for accessibility according to W3C guidelines. Many programs, some for cost, others free, are available to web page designers for accessibility. Free programs for checking accessibility of web pages and/or making them more accessible:

A-Prompt Toolkit, produced by the University of Toronto Adaptive Technology Resource Centre, is a method for checking web site accessibility. This software follows W3C guidelines. It evaluates HTML web pages for accessibility and provides solutions to make these pages accessible. All available at this web site: http://websitetips.com/accessibility/tools/.

CSE HTML Validator Lite version 9.02 is a free online checker for Windows that checks web pages for Section 508 compliance. The free version is also a spellchecker, changes tags to lower case, places automatic quotation marks, and removes HTML tags from documents. This product has a for-cost version that is a powerful, professional tool checking JavaScript, CSS, PHP, and links and accessibility (http://freehtmlvalidator.com).

Adobe PDF Access Utility is a free download and converts PDF files to ASCII or HTML for people with visual handicaps to enable screen reader access.

The WAVE Accessibility Center, a program similar to BOBBY, checks for W3C and 508 compliance. This is an excellent tool for evaluating library web sites for accessibility.

Lynx viewer: This is a check for accessibility that simulates the Lynx text-only browser. The Lynx is an older, free, open-source browser. For browsing, links may be numbered or highlighted. This browser is still useful when slow dial-up connections are used.

WebXACT is a free program for checking individual web pages for accessibility.

ALTERNATIVE ACCESS SYSTEMS

Technology has come a long way from a few decades ago when all that was available was Braille reading material, books on LP records, and large print books. Now many more options in the form of electronic materials make it possible not only for the individuals with visual disabilities to function better but offer convenience for sighted people who may want to listen to a book, which they have downloaded into PDAs or cell phones, while driving a car. Books may be downloaded to personal computers through organizations like Bookshare.org and web Braille from NLS as well as timely materials like newspapers, magazines, and journal articles. Many different kinds of digital talking book players are also available such as Victor Classic, Plexor, Book Port, BookCourier, and what are essentially CD players like Telex Scholar.[11]

Microsoft made available "Save as DAISY XML," a free program that works on Office 2003, 2007, 2010, and Word processor to save XML documents in DAISY multimedia format and is ideal for those people with print disabilities. The DAISY Pipeline and the Save as XML working together are a leap forward in universal information access for many people.

CLOSED CIRCUIT TV

There are many different types of reading machines in all price ranges. Some units are prohibitive in price for individuals but may not be cost prohibitive for a library or school environment. All of these machines convert printed material into sound or Braille using optical character recognition.

CCTV technology is not new but remains an important technology for people with limited vision. The CCTV unit contains a monitor with a video camera that captures the image of the page being read. It has variable enlargement and contrast capabilities. CCTV enables the user to write and read what is written in real time. CCTV units may be purchased in portable units. The newer units will fit inside a purse or briefcase. CCTV is simple technology and ideal for libraries and those who are not technically astute.

An example of CCTV is MERLIN, a lightweight desktop unit. MERLIN has auto focus, seven view modes, and memory for preferred settings. MERLIN is available from http://www.nanopac.com/Merlin%20Color.htm in color, black and white, and computer interfaced.

The HUMANWARE pocket viewer is a portable CCTV unit. It is available from NanoPac, Inc. It has a black and white or color monitor and a self-contained writing stand.

The OPTELEK "Traveler" provides portable magnification. It is very small and easy to use. It can be positioned upright for easy writing. It is only about 6.4 inches diagonal. OPTELEK vision products are based on CCTV technology and provide powerful magnification capability.

AcroBat is a CCTV with up to 65x magnification from NanoPac, Inc. The camera angle may be changed for writing or reading—http://www .nanopac.com/Buy%20Online.htm.

SCREEN READERS

Low Vision Software: Zoom Text, MAGic, and Dolphin

Zoom Text is screen-reading software that magnifies web sites and any other computer functions. MAGic-low vision is software for magnifying the computer screen. Dolphin Supernova is a software screen reader/magnifier with Braille support. It supports multiple screens, has a variety of color options, and can be used by people with partial sight or those who are totally blind. It covers a variety of vision disabilities.

Window Eyes 7.01 GW Micro Screen Reader for Windows has voice synthesizer compatibility. Window Eyes 7.01 GW Micro Screen Reader for

Windows is compatible with Windows 98 to Vista to Windows 7. It is compatible with Internet, e-mail, word processing. The unit uses a speech synthesizer to read aloud the keyboard input as well as graphic icons and dialog boxes. It reads highlighted text and has Braille support.

Low Vision

Self-Contained Desktop Units

SARA is a scanning and reading appliance that is essentially self-contained. SARA connects to a monitor. This unit is compatible with DAISY format and may be used with little or no instruction.

The POET Reading Machine is a self-contained reading machine that is easy to use and requires no training, excellent for those who are not comfortable using a computer.

The PLUSTEK reading machine is self-contained, similar to the POET but much cheaper. The PLUSTEK is distributed by LSS Products—http://www.lssproducts.com. E-mail: info@lssproducts.com.

SOFTWARE DESIGNED TO TURN SCANNERS INTO READING MACHINES

CICERO text reader—http://www.yourdolphin.com.
E-mail: info@dolphinusa.com.
Enablemart is distributor—http://www.enablemart.com.
E-mail: sales@enablemart.com.
This complete Reading System works with laptops as well as desktops with scanners. CICERO is activated by using just a single key. The text may be enlarged upto 400%. The manufacturer is Premier Assistive Technology—http://www.readingmadeez.com.
E-mail: info@readingmadeeasy.com.
Distributor Next Generation Technologies, Inc.—http://www.ngtvoice.com.
E-mail: edward@ngtvoice.com.
The EZ VIP Reading System is adjustable for the individual user but then requires only two input buttons to run the program—http://www.jbliss.com.
E-mail: info@jbliss.com, manufacturer JBliss Imaging Systems.

CELL PHONES FOR THE BLIND

KnfbReader Mobile (Kurzweil NFB)

This cell-phone camera photographs text converting it to voice output and reads currency. Information saves and transfers to the computer or Braille note taker. This Nokia phone has web-browsing capability, GPS, e-mail, and MP3 capabilities. Nokia requires the purchase of a separate phone screen reader for these added functions. Ordinarily, its cost would make its addition in this book prohibitive, but it is included because it is such an impressive advance in technology. Knfb Reading Technology Inc. is the manufacturer with several distributors.

OWASYS 22C

OWASYS 22C is a relatively new cell phone for the blind available from the Spanish company Owasys. This phone does not have a display but provides audio output via a speech synthesizer.[12]

COMPLETE COMPUTER SYSTEMS FOR LOW VISION NEEDS

The Librette Turnkey System PC comes with monitor, printer, low vision software OCR with speech output, VIP Scan/Read/Write. It has over 600 books on CD. The Libra has added Zoom text. It is available at JBliss Imaging Systems—http://www.knfbreader.com.

Voice Recognition Laptop and Desktop—These complete computer systems are available from AbilityNet. They have voice recognition technology already installed and the computer is ready to use.

Reader Magnifier Laptop and Desktop units are outfitted with screen enlarging software for those who need magnification and a screen reader. They are available from AbilityNet.

Packages for seniors from Microsoft: these HP computers are ready to use with basic software installation already in place and are especially useful for people who have little confidence with using computers. Either desktop or laptops are available, with choice of what the user wants and includes a printer (www.enablemart.com).

Freeware

Free technology is available free from many web sites. Many of these are either duplicated or similar products already available, for instance, in Microsoft XP, Vista, and Windows 7. Many of the free products are helpful but have limited applications. The products we chose for this book appear to be useful and more versatile.

Emacspeak (emacspeak.sourceforge.net/) is a free downloadable speech interface for visually impaired computer users. Emacspeak speaks aloud specific printed information. For example, an ordinary screen reader would read only numbers, but the Emac actually reads a date. A virtual spatial layout is created by using sound icons.

FATBITS is a screen magnifier for Windows XP free for downloading (www.digitalmantra.com/fatbits/). This magnifier enlarges a part of the screen around the mouse area in a separate window. It is great especially for web designers who want to see down to pixel level. Background colors can be changed to make viewing more comfortable depending on need. The pixels may be either visible or hidden. It has the ability to smooth outlines of letters. It works with different monitors and is written in "C."

WordTalk (www.wordtalk.org.uk/) is a free text-to-speech software for use with Microsoft Word upwards from Word 97. Conveniences are being able to change highlighter colors and voices. There is a toolbar giving the user a choice of what is read from the screen: following the cursor, the individual word, sentence, or paragraph. WordTalk also has a talking spellchecker. It has keyboard shortcuts, is compatible with voices already on the computer, and allows the reading rate to be adjusted. This is ideal for people with reading difficulties. These are some similar features with the Kurzweil 3000.

Sayz Me (www.datafurnace.net.au/sayzme/) is a free text-to-speech reader designed for Windows 98 or later. The voice can be adjusted for pitch and speed, text is highlighted as it is spoken and may be adjusted for color and font type. It was updated in 2007. Text can be typed into the system or cut and copied into it.

ReadPlease 2003 (www.readplease.com) is a free text to speech software for Windows. There is also a for-cost version ReadPlease Plus 3000. The voices are Microsoft Mike, Mary and Sam with adjustable speed and color contrast options. The Plus version also is able to forward and backward and highlight text as it is being read. It offers more choice of voices and languages.

AMIS 3.1 (Adaptive Multimedia Information System) (www.daisy.org/amis) is a free software program with multi-language capability for reading DAISY 2.02 and DAISY 3 standard books.

Free Cursor is a free cursor enlarger that is available from http://rbx.de/big-cursors/ for Windows with instructions in English and German.

MouseCam 1 is a free magnifier that enlarges anything around the cursor up to 20x for Windows 95 and up. It is available from www.soft32.com/download_7870.html.

MyFTC (My Freedom to Communicate) is a free download text-to-speech program for Windows that enables people who have trouble speaking to communicate, available from http://www.oatsoft.org/Software/myftc.

NaturalReader 9 is a free text to speech reader with a Microsoft voice that can also convert text files to MP3 files for iPods. NaturalReader 9 is available at http://www.naturalreaders.com/.

PodioBooks is a free source for book downloads available from http://www.podiobooks.com/.

SUITEKeys 1.0 for Microsoft Windows 95, 98, NT 4.0, and 2000/XP is available at www.cs.cofc.edu/~manaris/SUITEKeys/. This is an open source speech recognition system to operate a Windows environment computer.

Ultra Hal Text-to-Speech Reader is a free screen reader that reads typed words and is available at download.cnet.com/Ultra-Hal.../3000-7239 _4-10071733.html. Ultra Hal works with Windows 95, Windows 98, Me, 2000XP, 2003, Vista, and NT.

ZenKEY 2.0.5 is a free download that enables the user to control the computer with keystrokes and mouse. Programs and documents may open using this software. It is available at download.cnet.com/ZenKEY/3000-2317 _4-10376343.html.

Dasher is a free software program that enables people who are able to use a mouse but not a keyboard to choose letters that stream across a computer screen. The user points at the letters with a mouse click and the program tries to guess the next letter or word. It is not meant for complicated writing but is useful for writing e-mails and letters. It is available at www .inference.phy.cam.ac.uk/dasher/DasherSummary.html.

SOFTWARE AND ALTERNATIVE INPUT DEVICES

The average computer keyboard, based on the model of the typewriter, is a simple system for data entry for people who know how to type. To those with print disabilities, however, the typewriter can be a barrier to the use of the computer. The keys are small and difficult to see for those with vision problems, and manual dexterity is required to use the mouse. People with motor problems are excluded from normal computer use. For many people an alternative information input system is required other than standard keyboard mouse. These people may be able to use large keyboards with large, easy to see letters. Some may benefit from an on-screen keyboard that is touch-sensitive and is designed to be used with a finger or mouth stick and mouse. Those who are paralyzed and have virtually no motor function may be able to control the computer by voice only. Many voice activation software programs are available. Keystrokes may be reprogrammed to suit needs of those with limited dexterity. Even Morse code input devices are available. The dwell time, or time the keystroke remains active, may be changed for those with tremors to ignore accidental keystrokes and keys can simulate mouse functions. Stickykeys enable those with motor disabilities to press computer keys in sequence instead of all at once like "cont-alt-del." Keyguards are available for those who have limited hand control. Keyguards protect the keyboard from inadvertent keystrokes. Many keyboards may be designed at home for specific functions with large print keyboards. A variety of custom and large-print keyboards designed for low vision are available.

OpenBook 8.0

OpenBook is OCR (optical character recognition) software available from Freedom Scientific. OpenBook converts scanned documents into electronic format like audio files where it may be saved as audio and transferred to iPod or MP3. OpenBook Works with Windows 2000, XP, Vista, and Windows 7. Appearance of the screen is set by the user for best viewing with font and color adjustable options. OpenBook supports DAISY and Braille. A scanner may be purchased separately. OpenBook is available at ... www.freedomscientific.com/.../fs/openbook-product-page.asp.

A free Windows on-screen keyboard is available at www.sharewarejunction .com/download/windows-onscreen-keyboard/.

MALTRON carries a variety of adaptive and ergonomic keyboards for special needs: single hand-keyboards, single fingerboards, and mouth-stick adapted computer entry for those people with print disabilities and motor impairments (http://www.maltron.com). The company is based in Surrey, UK.

IntelliKeys by IntelliTools is a membrane keyboard that has a choice of six different overlays for Macintosh or Windows computers. The overlays vary in keyboard configuration and high-contrast colors. The function and area of the keys can be changed to provide several larger keys. There are keyguards available separately for those with limited motor function. These keyboard adaptors are available at www.EnableMart.com/ Intellikeys.

One of the easiest ways to adapt the mouse for those with print disabilities is to make use of the features in the Microsoft Windows XP, Vista, and Windows 7 program and using the built-in on-screen keyboard. The screen is also navigable by using the arrow keys. Other alternative input devices are trackball mice and joysticks, switch and button control, head tracking devices or eye pointing devices, or even the newest brain-wave input. Another easy way to access computer function is by voice activation, also a built-in feature of Windows XP, Vista, and Windows 7. Voice activation is a great help for users with learning disabilities who benefit from a variety of sensory inputs.

BRAILLE EQUIPMENT

Braille translators take written pages and convert them to Braille files that may then be processed and printed in Braille.

The DBT Duxbury Braille Translator is a translation software. DBT 10.7 SR1 is now available. Duxbury takes files in various formats and translates them into Braille. The information appears on a computer screen and may be edited from there and embossed (http://www.duxburysystems.com/).

A free Braille translator is available at libbraille.org/translator.php.

BRAILLE TYPEWRITERS

Slate and Stylus Type Reading Machines

A slate and stylus is a manual Braille note-taking device. Braille dots are punched manually into a slate. It is probably the most simple note-taking device.

Information for this system is found at the following web site: ... www.nfb.org/images/nfb/Publications/fr/.../f130302.html.

ELECTRONIC NOTE-TAKING DEVICES

Braille Sense and Braille Sense Plus. This is a Braille notetaker available at Enablemart (http://www.enablemart.com/). It is lightweight and easy to carry, to be used instead of a laptop computer. It is a 32 Braille cell unit with speech capability. It includes DAISY player, Bluetooth, and optional wireless Internet connection and has many software programs available for it.

Braille embossing is a noisy process. There are sound enclosures available ideal for libraries that enable Braille users access to a printer without disturbing other patrons (www.brailler.com/other.htm).

Large Screen Keyboards—Keys-U-See available at www.keyconnection .com. Keyboards with large letters and high-contrast black-on-yellow and other colors are ideal for those needing some degree of vision help.

FrogPad is a single-hand keyboard to be used with portable gadgets like PDAs to make input more comfortable even for people with no disabilities. PDAs are available for right-hand or left-hand use (www.frogpad.com).

Dragon Dictate/Naturally Speaking Wake-up Keyboard is a keyboard from NanoPac, Inc. It is ideal for people who use a voice control exclusively for their computers. It has a simple microphone switch and eliminates inadvertent sleep/wakeup problems with the computer (http://www.nanopac .com/Wake%20up%20Keyboard.htm).

ALTERNATIVE MICE

Mice may be buttons, hand switches and tongue switches, infrared remote systems, trackballs, head trackers, joysticks, and speech input. Almost any needed input is available. Sip and puff switches can be adapted for Morse code input.

MICROSOFT TUTORIALS

There are many fine accessibility options designed for people with vision, mobility, hearing, and speech problems on the Microsoft computer software. The scope of this book permits only that we will concentrate on Windows XP, Vista, and Windows 7 and discuss only those features that will make the computer more easily usable by those people with disabilities. We will examine accessibility features for people with vision problems: icon size and font size, screen resolution, display appearance, contrast settings, magnifier, cursor size and cursor locator, cursor blink rate, and serial keys feature for alternative input devices. The assistive layout in Windows 7 is very similar to the assistive layout in the Vista program. A more detailed discussion and the Microsoft tutorials are available at www.microsoft.com/enable/. Screenshots are available on the Microsoft web site also.

Options for the Internet Explorer

In Windows XP, on "view" change the text size from smallest to largest. Then go to TOOLS—Internet options.

On the bottom of the "General" tab find colors, fonts, languages, and accessibility.

Under COLORS, set visited, unvisited, and hover color from a wide variety of choices.

Accessibility

In Windows XP, under accessibility, there is a choice of "ignore colors, fonts, or font size" specified on the web pages.

This allows formatting to a style sheet specified by the user.

Word Processor

Across the top of the screen in the word processor click on "view." This allows enlarging the text and shows what the enlargement will look like.

Zoom option on "view" allows for changing text size up to 500 percent.

Accessibility Wizard

It is important to understand that the assistive technology functions in Microsoft Windows XP, Vista, and Windows 7 are accessible through several different paths. One of the easiest modules to work with is the Accessibility Wizard. It is accessed through Start–All Programs–Accessories–Accessibility–Accessibility Wizard. The Wizard contains a group of assistive devices but makes setup easy by asking the user questions about their disability and enabling the user to choose from vision, hearing, or mobility options.

The first window provides a choice of three different sizes of print. The user chooses small, medium, or large print or icons.

The next page gives the option of choosing larger print in menus and the option of turning on the magnifier.

Varying Color/Contrast Scheme, Icon, Size, and Scroll Bar Size

The varying color/contrast scheme, icon size, and scroll bar size page offers a choice of individual areas of difficulty-seeing, hearing, mobility, and administrative options. It enables the Wizard program to customize the computer depending on the choice made here: for instance, if "I am blind or have difficulty seeing things on screen," the next page allows change of scroll bar size.

The next page gives a choice of three different icon sizes.

The next page gives a choice of four different color scheme combinations that allows the user to vary the contrast quite dramatically. Previews of the color schemes are given.

Changing Cursor Size

The next page allows a choice of cursor size and color choice of black, white, or inverting. One of these options may make it easier to see the cursor.

The next page offers sliders for the cursor blink rate and cursor width.

The last page shows what changes have been made.

Individual Assistive Modules in Windows XP.

Magnifier

The magnifier is available under "Start-all programs-accessories-accessibility."

Choose Magnifier. The magnifier appears on the top half of the screen but its location on the screen may be changed by drag-and-click.

On the bottom next to the START a bar with "Magnifier Setting" appears.

Magnifier setting enables level of magnification and where you want the focus to be—either follow the cursor, the keyboard, or edit text. Contrast may also be changed here with the "invert colors" option.

With the magnification above five, the letters are no longer smooth.

The magnifier is not as powerful as those available at-cost, but it does offer some level of help for those who need only a little bit of help. If the magnifier is combined with the 500 percent zoom on the word processor, the magnification is quite powerful. See accessing the magnifier setting. www.microsoft.com/enable/.

Start–All Programs–Accessories–Accessibility– NARRATOR

This options turns on the narrator. It is a limited program that reads aloud dialog boxes that are clicked on and individual letters that are typed, including punctuation. It announces events on the screen. Narrator gives a choice of three voices, speed, and pitch of voices but cannot be used as a document reader.

ON-SCREEN KEYBOARD

The on-screen keyboard is accessed through Start-All Programs-Accessories-Accessibility-On-Screen Keyboard.

The on-screen keyboard is small but is useful with the screen magnifier.

The "keyboard" setting on the keyboard allows choice of enhanced or standard keyboard and regular or block letter layout, and a choice of the number of keys.

Enhanced keyboard contains the number panel.

The "settings" option under "keyboard" allows click sound, font choice, and type size.

"Typing mode" under "settings" permits choice of click, hover, or joystick to select letters.

The UTILITY MANAGER from All Programs—Start–Accessories–Accessibility–Utility Manager shows whether the on-screen narrator, magnifier are running and the option of starting these utilities as soon as the computer is turned on. This is very useful because it allows the individual user's choices of assistive technology to be remained turned on or off.

CURSOR OPTIONS

The cursor is enlarged through the Control Panel-Mouse option.

There is a wide variety of pointer types and sizes available.

Under Pointers-Scheme a great variety of pointers becomes available, including animated pointers. Pointers may be enlarged or color-inverted to make them easier to see.

A useful option is to show the location of the pointer: when the "control" key is pressed. Visibility increases by clicking the option to follow the pointer trail.

Speed of pointer may be changed at this module.

Another handy feature is the "Click lock" also accessed through the mouse module in the control panel that allows the mouse to be clicked and dragged without depressing the mouse button. A brief click turns this feature on and off.

The buttons may reconfigure to "right" or "left" handed function.

Display Module

The Display module available under Start-Control Panel allows the option of changing Display properties (Control Panel–Display–Appearance). Here the Windows style, color scheme, and icon size may be chosen. On the

Settings Tab on the Display module, the screen resolution and color quality may be chosen. Lower screen resolution permits larger icons.

ACCESSIBILITY OPTIONS IN WINDOWS VISTA

Options for the Internet Explorer

On the top right, choose zoom in, zoom out, or percentage. Text size may also be enlarged here. On the bottom right of the screen is also a zoom sign where the print size may be changed to 400 percent or zoom in or out. Microsoft Vista's accessibility unit is the Ease of Access Center. It is available through Start–Programs–Accessories–Ease of Access Center. The magnifier, narrator, on-screen keyboard, or contrast settings may then be accessed, level of magnification may be changed, and colors inverted for high contrast. The narrator voices and speed may be changed.

The On-Screen keyboard, Narrator, and Speech Recognition may be accessed from this site. The computer suggests various setting depending on what areas the user needs assistance with: hearing, speech, learning, blindness, or low vision. It offers the option of computer settings for learning disability and speech impairment that Windows XP Wizard does not offer.

ASSISTIVE TECHNOLOGY (GLOSSARY)

Products compatible with Microsoft Windows operating systems, made by independent assistive technology manufacturers, are included in the Resources section. People having vision difficulties and impairments may be interested in the following assistive technology:

- **Screen enlargers** (or screen magnifiers) work like a magnifying glass. They enlarge a portion of the screen as the user moves the focus—increasing legibility for some users. Some screen enlargers allow a user to zoom in and out on a particular area of the screen.
- **Screen readers** are software programs that present graphics and text as speech. A screen reader is used to verbalize, or "speak," everything on the screen, including names and descriptions of control buttons, menus, text, and punctuation.
- **Speech recognition systems**, also called voice recognition programs, allow people to give commands and enter data using their voices rather than a mouse or keyboard.
- **Speech synthesizers** (often referred to as text-to-speech [TTS] systems) receive information going to the screen in the form of letters, numbers, and punctuation marks, and then "speak" it out loud. Using speech synthesizers allows blind users to review their input as they type.

- **Refreshable Braille displays** provide tactile output of information represented on the computer screen. The user reads the Braille letters with his or her fingers, and then, after a line is read, refreshes the display to read the next line.
- **Braille embossers** transfer computer-generated text into embossed Braille output. Braille translation programs convert text scanned in or generated via standard word processing programs into Braille, which can then be printed on the embosser.
- **Talking word processors** are software programs that use speech synthesizers to provide auditory feedback of what is typed.
- **Large-print word processors** allow the user to view everything in large text without added screen enlargement.

WEB RESOURCES

Ability Hub—http://abilityhub.com
Adobe—http://www.adobe.com
A–Z for DeafBlindness—www.deafblind.com
Assistive Technology—http://www.onlineconferencingsystems.com/at.htm#top
Assistive Technology (for web site developers)—http://websitetips.com/accessibility/
Canadian National Institute for the Blind—http://www.cnib.ca/en/Default.aspx
DO-IT (Disabilities, Opportunities, Internetworking and Technologies)—http://www.disabled-world.com/
Free and Inexpensive Assistive Technology Software—http://adaptech.dawsoncollege.qc.ca/fandi_enewwriting.php
National Library Service for the Blind and Physically Handicapped—http://www.loc.gov/nls/index.html
Open Source Assistive Technology—http://www.oatsoft.org/
Royal National Institute for the Blind—http://www.rnib.org.uk/xpedio/groups/public/documents/code/InternetHome.hcsp
Side by Side WCAG vs. 508—http://www.jimthatcher.com/sidebyside.htm#WCAG
WebAIM TEITAC—http://webaim.org/teitac/
W3C-web Accessibility Initiative—http://www.w3.org/

PRINT DISABILITY AND VISION RESOURCES

Hardware

Accessible Graphing Calculator (ViewPlus Technologies, Inc.)—http://www.viewplus.com/solutions/math-access/
Alva 570 Satellite Pro Braille Display (Vision Cue)—http://www.synapseadaptive.com/alva/alva_pro/alva_570_satellite_pro.htm
AspireReader (CAST)—http://www.axistive.com/aspirereader-4-0.html
Blind/Low Vision Group—http://www.lowvisionsolutions.com/topaz/adwords-B.html?gclid=CMy54LSXj6ICFY1a2godV0LQaw

Book Wizard Reader (American Printing House for the Blind [APH])—http://book
-wizard-reader.software.informer.com/1.3/download/

Braille BookMaker, Express 100, Express 150 (By Enabling Technologies Company)—
http://www.brailler.com/ftp/brlx.pdf

Cicero Text Reader (Dolphin Computer Access Inc.)—http://www.yourdolphin.com/
productdetail.asp?id=14

Complete Reading System (Premier Assistive Technology)—http://www.ngtvoice
.com/products/software/ocr/crs.htm

Connect Outloud web Access (Freedom Scientific, Inc.)—http://www.freedomscientific
.com/fs_downloads/connect.asp

DigiCite (Compusult Limited)—http://www.hear-it.com/DigiCite_broc_060103.pdf

Disabled World—http://www.disabled-world.com/

DocReader (T & I [Technology & Integration])—http://www.zoomtext.com/videos/
Tutorial/Features/DocReader.html

Dolphin Producer (Dolphin Computer Access Inc.)—http://www.axistive.com/
dolphin-producer-to-solve-learning-disabilities.html.

Dolphin Tutor (Dolphin Computer Access Inc.)—http://www.yourdolphin.com/
productdetail.asp?id=13

DyslexiWrite (SecondGuess Software)—http://www.synapseadaptive.com/dyslexiwrite/
index.htm

EASI, Equal Access to Software and Information—http://people.rit.edu/easi/

EasyType Large Print PS/2 Beige Keyboard (DataCal Enterprises)—https://www
.renki.wpcomp.com/~ulmaster/Online-Store/Keyboards-Pointing-Devices/
easytype-beige.htm

Elotype 4E (Blista-Brailletec)—http://www.igi-group.com/shop/product.php
?id_product=77

ET (Enabling Technologies Company)—http://www.brailler.com/

Eurotype/E (Blista-Brailletec)—http://www.igi-group.com/shop/product.php
?id_product=76

Flexiboard (ZYGO Industries, Inc.)—http://www.google.com/search?q=EZ+Keys
&rls=com.microsoft:en-us:IE-SearchBox&ie=UTF-8&oe=UTF-8&sourceid
=ie7&rlz=1I7GGLL_en

Impacto Texto (Blista-Brailletec)—http://brailletec.de/impactoe.pdf

IVEO (ViewPlus Technologies, Inc.)—http://www.viewplus.com/solutions/touch
-audio-learning/

JAWS for Windows Screen Reading Software (Freedom Scientific, Inc.)—http://
www.freedomscientific.com/products/fs/jaws-product-page.asp

Juliet Classic, Juliet Pro, Juliet Pro 60 Interpoint Printer (Enabling Technologies)—
http://www.brailler.com/juli1.htm

Keyguards (Turning Point Therapy and Technology, Inc.)—http://www
.turningpointtechnology.com/KG/KGMGMain.asp

Learn Keys (American Printing House for the Blind [APH])—http://tech.aph.org/lk
_info.htm

LookOUT Professional (Sensory Software)—http://www.sensorysoftware.com/
free.html

Magic Touch (KEYTEC, Inc.)—http://www.magictouch.com/

Magni-Cam (By Innoventions, Inc.)—http://www.magnicam.com/

Magnify OUTLOUD (Colligo Corp.)—http://www.turningpointtechnology.com/Vision/CG/Magnify%20OutLoud.htm

Marathon Brailler (Enabling Technologies Company)—http://www.afb.org/prodProfile.asp?ProdID=30&SourceID=45

Money Talks (American Printing House for the Blind [APH])—http://www.aph.org/products/mt_bro.html

OFF Limits (Premier Assistive Technology)—http://www.tcnj.edu/~technj/2004/premierat.htm

OpenBook Scanning and Reading Software (Freedom Scientific, Inc.)—http://www.freedomscientific.com/products/fs/openbook-product-page.asp

Optelec ClearView+ (Optelec US, Inc.)—http://www.optelec.com/en_US/product/clearview+-series

PC Talking Typing Tutor (Rehabilitation Technology Services)—http://www.google.com/search?q=PC+Talking+Typing+Tutor&rls=com.microsoft:en-us:IE-SearchBox&ie=UTF-8&oe=UTF-8&sourceid=ie7&rlz=1I7GGLL_en

PDF Magic (Premier Assistive Technology)—http://www.magicpdf.com/magicpdf.html

Paragon Braille Embosser (HumanWare)—http://www.synapseadaptive.com/braille.htm

Plate Embossing Device PED-30 (Enabling Technologies Company)—http://www.brailler.com/ped30.htm

Porta-Thiel (Blista-Brailletec)—http://www.abledata.com/abledata.cfm?pageid=113583&top=0&productid=76188&trail=0

Premier CD/DVD Creator (Premier Assistive Technology)—https://secure2.convio.net/psb/site/Ecommerce/500384322?VIEW_PRODUCT=true&product_id=2737&store_id=1101

ReadText (Colligo Corp.)—http://www.innosolu.com/Scan%20N%20Talk.html

Romeo 25, Romeo Pro 50 (Enabling Technologies Company)—http://www.brailler.com/ftp/rb2550user.pdf

Scan and Read Pro (Premier Assistive Technology)—http://www.readingmadeez.com/products/scanreadpro.html

StreetTalk GPS Solution (Freedom Scientific, Inc., Blind/Low Vision Group)—http://www.freedomscientific.com/products/fs/streettalk-gps-product-page.asp

Talking Checkbook (Premier Assistive Technology)—http://www.readingmadeez.com/products/TalkingCheckbook.html

Talking Screen (Words+, Inc.)—http://www.words-plus.com/website/pdf_files/tswin.pdf

Talking Toolbox (MarvelSoft Enterprises, Inc.)—http://www.braillebookstore.com/view.php?C=Talking+Toolbox+for+Windows

Talking Typer (American Printing House for the Blind [APH])—http://tech.aph.org/tt_info.htm

Talking Typing Teacher (MarvelSoft Enterprises, Inc.)—http://www.braillebookstore.com/view.php?C=Talking+Typing+Teacher+for+Windows

Tech/Syms (Advanced Multimedia Devices Inc.)—http://www.spectronicsinoz.com/product/techsyms

Text-to-Audio (Premier Assistive Technology)—http://www.premierathome.com/support/Manuals/Text-To-Audio%20Manual.doc

Ultimate Talking Dictionary (Premier Assistive Technology)—http://download
.cnet.com/Ultimate-Talking-Dictionary/3000-2279_4-10286049.html

Software

AceReader (Stepware, Inc.)—http://www.acereader.com/

Biggy (RJ Cooper and Associates)—http://www.rjcooper.com/biggy-light/index.html

Captain's Log: Attention Skills Developmental (BrainTrain, Inc.)—http://www
.braintrain.com/professionals/captains_log/captainslog_nextgen_pro.htm

Connect Outloud web Access Software (Freedom Scientific, Inc.)—http://www
.freedomscientific.com/fs_downloads/connect.asp

CubeWriter (MK Technologies)—http://www.cubewriter.com/

Discover 1.8 software (Madentec Limited)—http://www.hmc-nv.be/index.php?id=125

DocReader (T & I [Technology & Integration])—http://www.zoomtext.com/videos/
Tutorial/Features/DocReader.html

Dragon NaturallySpeaking Professional (Nuance Communications, Inc.)—http://
shop.nuance.com/store/nuanceus/Content/pbPage.dns-page1

Duxbury Braille Translators (Duxbury Systems, Inc.)—http://www.duxburysystems
.com/product2.asp?product=DBT%20Win&level=major&action=demo

EasePublisher—DAISY Authoring Software (Dolphin Computer Access)—http://
www.nattiq.com/en/node/79

eClipseWriter DAISY Digital Talking Book Creator (Innovative Rehabilitation Technology, Inc.)—http://www.yourdolphin.com/productdetail.asp?id=12

English Braille American Edition (Opus Technologies)—http://www.brailleauthority
.org/update07.html

Eurotype/E (Blista-Brailletec)—http://www.igi-group.com/shop/product.php
?id_product=76

EZ Keys (Words+, Inc.)—http://www.gokeytech.com/e_z_keys.htm

Flexiboard (ZYGO Industries, Inc.)—http://www.zygo-usa.com/flexi.html

FSReader DAISY Player (Freedom Scientific, Inc., Blind/Low Vision Group)—http://
www.freedomscientific.com/products/fs/fsreader-product-page.asp

GOODFEEL Braille Music Translator (Dancing Dots Braille Music Tech.)—http://
www.dancingdots.com/main/goodfeel.htm

Gus! Big Cursor (Gus Communications, Inc.)—http://www.gusinc.com/
computeraccess.html

Hal (Dolphin Computer Access Inc.)—http://www.halcomm.com/

Impacto Texto (Blista-Brailletec)—http://brailletec.de/impactoe.pdf

IVEO (ViewPlus Technologies, Inc.)—http://www.viewplus.com/solutions/touch
-audio-learning/

JAWS for Windows Screen Reading Software (Freedom Scientific, Inc.)—http://
www.freedomscientific.com/products/fs/jaws-product-page.asp

Juliet Classic, Juliet Pro, Juliet Pro 60 Interpoint Printer (Enabling Tech.)—http://
www.synapseadaptive.com/brailler/br/juliet_pro.htm

Keyguards (Turning Point Therapy and Technology, Inc.)—http://www.infogrip
.com/product_view.asp?RecordNumber=940

Kurzweil Educational Systems, Inc.—http://www.kurzweiledu.com/

Learn Keys (American Printing House for the Blind (APH)—http://www.aph.org/
products/learnkey.html

Lime Aloud (Dancing Dots Braille Music Technology)—http://www.dancingdots
.com/prodesc/limealoud.htm

Lunar Screen Magnifier (Dolphin Computer Access Inc.)—http://www.yourdolphin
.com/productdetail.asp?id=3

MAGic Screen Magnification, Standard and Professional (Freedom Scientific, Inc.,
Blind/Low Vision Group)—http://www.freedomscientific.com/products/lv/
magic-bl-product-page.asp

Magic Touch (KEYTEC, Inc.)—http://www.magictouch.com/

Magni-Cam (By Innoventions, Inc.)—http://www.magnicam.com/

Magnify OUTLOUD (Colligo Corp.)—http://www.turningpointtechnology.com/
Vision/CG/Magnify%20OutLoud.htm

Marathon Brailler (Enabling Technologies Company)—http://www.afb.org/
prodProfile.asp?ProdID=30&SourceID=45

Money Talks (American Printing House for the Blind [APH])—http://www.aph.org/
products/mt_bro.html

OFF Limits (Premier Assistive Technology)—http://www.tcnj.edu/~technj/2004/
premierat.htm

OpenBook Scanning and Reading Software (Freedom Scientific, Inc.)—http://
www.freedomscientific.com/products/fs/openbook-product-page.asp

Optelec ClearView+ (Optelec US, Inc.)—http://www.optelec.com/en_US/product/
clearview+-series

Opus Braille Font Pack (Opus Technologies)—http://www.opustec.com/products/
fontpack/index.html

PC Talking Typing Tutor (Rehabilitation Technology Services)—http://
www.talktypetutor.com/

PDF Magic (Premier Assistive Technology)—http://www.readingmadeez.com/products/
PDFMagicPro.html

Paragon Braille Embosser (HumanWare)—http://www.synapseadaptive.com/
braille.htm

Perky Duck (Duxbury Systems, Inc.)—http://www.duxburysystems.com/freeware.asp

Plate Embossing Device PED-30 (Enabling Technologies Company)—http://
www.almispah.net/EN_Production%20Braille%20Embossers%20PED-30.htm

PnC Net (JBliss Low Vision Systems)—http://www.jbliss.com/pncNet.html

PointSmart (Infogrip, Inc.)—http://www.infogrip.com/product_view.asp?Record
Number=988

Porta-Thiel (Blista-Brailletec)—http://www.abledata.com/abledata.cfm?pageid
=113583&top=0&productid=76188&trail=0

Premier CD/DVD Creator (Premier Assistive Technology)—https://secure2
.convio.net/psb/site/Ecommerce/500384322?VIEW_PRODUCT=true&product
_id=2737&store_id=1101

REACH Interface Author (Applied Human Factors, Inc.)—http://www.ahf-net.com/
reach.htm

REACH Scan Plus Lists (Applied Human Factors, Inc.)—http://www.ahf-net.com/
reach_scan_plus.htm

REACH with Smart Keys (Applied Human Factors, Inc.)—http://www.spectronicsinoz
.com/product/21171

ReadText (Colligo Corp.)—https://wisdomware.com/catalog/product_info.php
?cPath=52&products_id=259&osCsid=dtns5bj06lve729netv2nmaf22

Reading Bar for Internet Explorer (ReadPlease Corp.)—http://www.readplease.com/english/readingbar.php

Romeo 25, Romeo Pro 50 (Enabling Technologies Company)—http://www.brailler.com/ftp/rb2550user.pdf

Scan and Read Pro (Premier Assistive Technology)—http://www.readingmadeez.com/products/scanreadpro.html

Scan N Talk Ultra (Colligo Corp.)—http://www.enablemart.com/Catalog/Low-Vision-Scanners/Scan-N-Talk-Ultra

2nd Speech Center (Zero2000 Software)—http://www.zero2000.com/

SoothSayer Scan Plus (Applied Human Factors, Inc.)—http://www.ahf-net.com/Product%20List.htm

SoothSayer Word Prediction (Applied Human Factors, Inc.)—http://www.ahf-net.com/sooth.htm

StreetTalk GPS Solution (Freedom Scientific, Inc., Blind/Low Vision Group)—http://www.freedomscientific.com/products/fs/streettalk-gps-product-page.asp

Studio Recorder (American Printing House for the Blind (APH)—http://tech.aph.org/sr_info.htm

Supernova Reader Magnifier Standard and Professional (Dolphin Computer Access, Inc.)—http://www.synapseadaptive.com/dolphin/supernova.htm

Talking Checkbook (Premier Assistive Technology)—http://www.enablemart.com/Talking-Checkbook

Talking Screen (Words+, Inc.)—http://www.words-plus.com/websiteweb site/pdf_files/tswin.pdf

Talking Toolbox (MarvelSoft Enterprises, Inc.)—http://www.braillebookstore.com/view.php?C=Talking+Toolbox+for+Windows

Talking Typer (American Printing House for the Blind (APH)—http://tech.aph.org/tt_info.htm

Talking Typing Teacher (MarvelSoft Enterprises, Inc.)—http://www.braillebookstore.com/view.php?C=Talking+Typing+Teacher+for+Windows

Tech/Syms (Advanced Multimedia Devices Inc.)—http://www.spectronicsinoz.com/product/techsyms

Text-to-Audio (Premier Assistive Technology)—http://www.premierathome.com/support/Manuals/Text-To-Audio%20Manual.doc

Ultimate Talking Dictionary (Premier Assistive Technology)—http://www.premierathome.com/products/UltimateTalkingDictionary.php

UltraKey (Bytes of Learning, Incorporated)—http://www.learningservicesus.com/home/ls2/page_4642/ultrakey_5.0_the_ultimate_keyboarding_tutor_standa.html

Verbal View of Windows XP (American Printing House for the Blind (APH)—http://tech.aph.org/vxp_info.htm

Verbal View of Word (American Printing House for the Blind [APH])—http://shop.aph.org/webapp/wcs/stores/servlet/Product_Verbal%20View%20of%20Word%20-%20ON%20SALE_D-10510-00P_10001_11051

Victor Reader Soft (HumanWare)—http://www.humanware.com/en-usa/home

VIP (Scan/Read/Write Software) (JBliss Low Vision Systems)—http://www.jbliss.com/Systems.html

The vOICe Learning Edition: Seeing with Your Ears (Peter Meijer)—http://www.seeingwithsound.com/

WinBraille (Sighted Electronics)—http://www.indexbraille.com/

Window-Eyes Professional (GW Micro, Inc.)—http://www.ulva.com/Online-Store/
    Screen-Reading/window-eyes.htm
Winkline (Speech Systems for the Blind)—http://www.oocities.com/hotsprings/villa/
    6113/art2.htm
Z Keys (Words+, Inc.)—http://caineassociates.com/products/index.php?main_page
    =index&manufacturers_id=36

NOTES

1. Rhea Joyce Rubin, "Planning for Library Services to People with Disabilities,"
Chicago, IL: Association of Specialized and Cooperative Library Agencies, American
Library Association (2001), quoted by Mary Ann Epp, "Closing the 95% Gap: Library
Resource Sharing for People with Print Disabilities," *Library Trends*, 3 (Winter 2006):
411–429, www.thefreelibrary.com (April 16, 2009).

2. Elizabeth Tank and Carsten Frederiksen, "The Daisy Standard: Entering the Global
Virtual Library," in *Library Trends*, March 22, 2007, http://ecnext.com/coms2/brows-
e_R_L016, April 24, 2009.

3. Canadian Library Association Working Group to Define the National Network for
Equitable Library Service (2005), "Opening the Book: A Business Plan for the National
Network for Equitable Library Service for Canadians with Print Disabilities," Ottawa,
ON, http://www.cla.ca/issues/NNELS_FINAL_EN, quoted by Mary Anne Epp, "Closing
the 95% Gap: Library Resource Sharing for People with Print Disabilities," *Library
Trends*, 3 (Winter 2006): 411–429, www.thefreelibrary.com (April 16, 2009).

4. Forrester Research, Inc., "Findings about Working Age Adults," 2003, Updated
February 14, 2008, http://www.micrsoft.com (April 6, 2009).

5. Canadian Library Association Working Group to Define the National Network for
Equitable Library Service (2005), "Opening the Book: A Business Plan for the National
Network for Equitable Library Service for Canadians with Print Disabilities," Ottawa,
ON, http://www.cla.ca/issues/NNELS_FINAL_EN, quoted by Mary Anne Epp, "Closing
the 95% Gap: Library Resource Sharing for People with Print Disabilities," *Library
Trends*, 3 (Winter 2006): 411–429, www.thefreelibrary.com (April 16, 2009).

6. Barbara T. Mates, "Computer Technology to Aid Special Audiences," in *Library
Technology Reports* (ALA: May/June 2006): 11. http://www.ala.org/Template.cfm?Section
=archive&template=conten.

7. www.daisy.org "Daisy NISO Standard—Structure Guidelines," Revised 2008
(April 24, 2009).

8. Peter Verhoefen, "WC3 web Standard Defines Accessibility for Next Generation
web," December 12, 2008, http://magnifiers.org/news.php?action=fullnews&id=355
(April 19, 2009).

9. Axel Schmetzke and David Comeaux, "Web Accessibility Trends in University
Libraries and Library Schools," in *Library Tech* 25 (2007): 457–477, (April 20, 2009).

10. Dey Alexander and Scott Ripon, "University Website Accessibility Revisited," Aus-
web 07, The Thirteenth Australian World Wide Web Conference (April 19, 2009).
www.ausweb.scu.edu.au/aw07/papers/refereed/alexander/index.htm, dey@deyalexander
.com, au scott@deyalexander.com.au.

11. Deborah Kendrick, "How Do I Read Thee? A Librarian Expands the Ways," AFB
5 (2004), www.afb.org (April 17, 2009).

12. www.gizmodo.com/007950/new-cellphone-for-the blind-from-owasys, Gizmodo
Gadget Blog, 2003, editor Jason Chen Nov 2003 (April 18, 2009).

CHAPTER 3

Mobility Disabilities

There are many different types of mobility disabilities and as many different definitions of mobility disabilities. Approximately one person in four has some sort of mobility disability.[1] Motor disabilities may be congenital—like cerebral palsy, or acquired during a disease process like amyotrophic lateral sclerosis (ALS) or multiple sclerosis (MS). Some of these diseases cause reduced vision or hearing along with mobility problems. Mobility disabilities may be the result of an automobile accident or workplace accident. Probably the most common type of mobility disability is that caused by age-related skeletal breakdown or by repetitive use injuries like carpal tunnel syndrome. Repetitive stress injuries account for approximately 60 percent of work-related injuries, with carpal tunnel syndrome being the most reported.[2]

It is difficult to judge on the surface just what kind of assistive technology someone with a mobility impairment might need. Often it is not a case of actual inability to perform a certain task but the experience of pain while performing the task. Assistive technology may be as all-encompassing as a head tracking device or speech recognition to access the computer, or as simple as an ergonomic keyboard to make typing easier or a trackball mouse for easier mouse input. Speech recognition may be an imperative for someone with a spinal cord injury or a convenience for someone who has never learned to type.

A clear path to the computer station can be an important first step in making the computer accessible for those with mobility impairments. Enough room must be available in the aisles for a wheelchair and the worktable must be adjustable to accommodate a wheelchair. The workstation area should conform to Americans with Disabilities (ADA) standards.

Persons with mobility problems may not have manual dexterity to operate an ordinary mouse. Many lack fine motor skills to choose screen options, thereby being excluded from real-time communications on the web. The keyboard is often a barrier to access for those with mobility impairments and one of the easiest barriers to overcome.

Keyguards, or covers for the keyboard, allow for more precise selection of letters and numbers for those who lack fine motor control skills. Special keyboards are available for use with a single hand, either left or right. These aids assist those people who have some motor control. Pointing devices, headsticks, or mouthsticks that replace keyboard function may work well with virtual keyboards for those with severe or total lack of mobility. Speech software (Dragon Naturally Speaking) or even Morse code may be used with off-on type switches or sip-n-puff switch.[3]

TALKING BOOKS

DAISY formatted books may be an answer for people who cannot turn the pages of an ordinary book. The "talking book" has been available for many years in the form of first phonograph records, then tape, and now digital. What makes the DAISY format unique is that these talking books may be navigated by informational material like chapters and the user may easily mark and revisit subjects throughout the book. DAISY users can read along with the audio, a great help for individuals with learning disabilities who benefit from a variety of sensory and mobility inputs.[4]

A new portable talking book is the Kindle from Amazon, new since 2007. It has over 270,000 books that may be downloaded for a fee. The new version, Kindle 2, also has a screen reader, but there is some controversy about whether it violates authors' copyrights for the audio book market.

FREEWARE

There is a lot of free software. Much of this software is not as good as commercial products but often does offer a significant amount of help. Microsoft's virtual keyboard is a free download for a PC by entering data with pointer or touch screen. It is available at http://download.cnet.com/1770-20_4-0.html? query=Microsoft+SideWinder+Virtual+Keyboard&searchtype=downloads.

AAC Keys is a free mouse emulation system for Microsoft Windows and Mac computers. A mouse emulation system is a software program that enables the user to substitute a button or a switch to provide a mouse click function instead of a standard mouse. An example is whereby a sensor (cursor) starts at the top of the page and keeps scanning until the user activates the switch at the desired object on the page. Keypad buttons may be used to move the cursor around, simulating mouse function.

AAC (Augmentative and Alternative Communication) is a charitable organization .www.aacinstitute.org/downloads/aackeys/AACKeys.html.

PointNClick mouse is a free on-screen virtual mouse that can be controlled with a trackball or any other pointer that works on screen, for people who have difficulty clicking an ordinary mouse. It works for Windows and Dos applications. This product is available at www.oatsoft.org/Software/pointnclick-mouse.

ClickAid 1.1.0 is a free on-screen mouse for people who have problems with switching between right and left mouse buttons or double clicking. It is available at freewareapp.com/clickaid_download/.

SUITEKeys v1.0 for Microsoft Windows 95, 98, NT 4.0, and 2000/XP (http://www.cs.cofc.edu/~manaris/SUITEKeys/). This free download is a speech recognition system instead of graphic interface for Microsoft Windows, enabling full computer function with voice only. This system was developed by the College of Charleston and the University of Louisiana at Lafayette.[5]

ZenKEY is a free download that enables the user to control the computer with using only keystrokes. Version 2.2.3 from 2010 is available at http://www.softpedia.com/get/System/Launchers-Shutdown-Tools/.

Dasher is a free software program that enables people who are able to use a mouse but not a keyboard to choose letters that stream across a computer screen. The user points at the letters with a mouse click and the program selects the next letter or word according to a probability system. Dasher is not intended for complicated writing but is useful for writing e-mails and letters. If text is being entered using speech, the user speaks the desired sequence of words into a speech recognition system, either Dragon Naturally Speaking or Microsoft speech engine.

A set of next possible word sequences is generated for the user to select one. Words that were missed by the program may be entered later and text may be corrected (http://www.inference.phy.cam.ac.uk/dasher/).

AUTO CORRECT FEATURE: The auto-correct feature in Microsoft allows short letter sequences to type standard text like an address. Auto correct settings allow repeated long words to be typed automatically.

FREE MOBILITY ASSISTIVE WARE IN WINDOWS XP, Vista, and Windows 7 (www.microsoft.com/enable).

Click lock: This enables the mouse to click and drag without having to hold the mouse button down.

Double-click speed: the user chooses the mouse click speed.

The mouse button can be programmed to reverse right and left functions.

StickyKeys is a keyboard assist for people with hand mobility problems: it enables pressing keys in sequence that normally require simultaneous input like control-alt-del.

FilterKeys: these are for people with hand tremors: keys may be set to enable unwanted repeated keystrokes.

MouseKeys: these enable the pointer to move with the keypad.

Character Repeat Rate—this is also good for those with hand tremors: set the speed of repetition of a character.

On-Screen Keyboard: enables use of external pointer or joystick for input.

For Windows Office Word Processor: Use Speech Module for dictation or use computer with voice commands.

VOICE COMMAND Voice Recognition–Kurzweil Voice, IBM Voice, Dragon Dictate.

For those who are not able to use a mouse or keyboard, voice command and voice recognition software is sophisticated voice-only access to the computer like Dragon Naturally Speaking. They work with either discrete or continuous speech. Continuous speech permits the user to dictate in a normal voice tone and correct errors later. Discrete speech systems require speaking one word at a time and word-by-word corrections. Voice recognition enables the spoken word to be converted to electronic format.

Free Microsoft Vista accessibility features for mobility problems are available at www.microsoft.com/enable.

Speech Recognition is a built-in feature of Vista that enables the user to use voice commands for computer and for dictation. It also enables voice-only e-mail and commands to operate the computer.

On-Screen Keyboard allows use of the joystick or other alternative input device.

Keyboard Shortcuts are a variety of keyboard commands that replace mouse input.

Mouse Keys move the mouse pointer with arrow keys.

Sticky Keys are similar to XP. Press keys in sequence instead of simultaneously.

Filter keys are similar to XP and aid people with hand tremors.

SerialKeys are NOT available in VISTA. It is suggested that AAC Keys or SKEYS be installed if needed.

ALTERNATIVE INPUT DEVICES FOR PEOPLE WITH MOBILITY DISABILITIES

The average computer keyboard, based on the model of the typewriter, is a simple system for data entry for most people who know how to type. Individuals with mobility disabilities, however, find typing to be a challenge or a barrier to the use of the computer. The keys are small and difficult to see for those with vision problems, and manual dexterity is required to use the mouse. People with motor problems are excluded from normal computer use. For many people an alternative information input system is required other than standard keyboard and mouse. Some may benefit from an on-screen keyboard that is touch-sensitive to be used with a finger or mouthstick and mouse. Those who are paralyzed and have virtually no motor function may be able to control the computer by voice only. Many software programs are available to make voice control typing possible. Dragon Naturally Speaking is only one of these. Keystrokes may be reprogrammed to suit the needs of those with limited dexterity. Even Morse code input devices are available. The dwell time may be changed for those with tremors to ignore accidental keystrokes and keys can simulate mouse functions. Dwell time is the amount of time the cursor remains active. Stickykeys enable those with motor disabilities to press computer keys in sequence instead of all at one "like cont-alt-del." Keyguards are available for those who have limited control of their hands. Keyguards protect the keyboard from inadvertent keystrokes.

ERGONOMIC KEYBOARDS

Ergonomic keyboards have made great advances in the past several years and many different designs are available. These keyboards are designed to reduce or eliminate pain in the parts of the hands, wrist, shoulders, and arms that are most likely to be affected by carpal tunnel syndrome and other repetitive stress injuries. Some people tend to use more force than necessary when pressing keys and some ergonomic keyboards are designed to be used with less force. Instead of all downward motions for pressing keys, some keys are designed to be pushed north, south, east, and west. Some ergonomic keyboards use finger motions that do not require carpal tunnel involvement. Ergonomic keyboards are made to be adjustable by the user to whatever is required for comfort. Many of these keyboards are programmable depending on user requirements.

People who use computer keyboards for many hours a day often hold their hands in unnatural (or non-neutral) positions, thereby putting unusual stress on muscles and tendons. Wrists are bent up and to the right and left and held there. This causes strain on the structures inside the wrist. If the keyboard is too high, elbows may be bent away from the body and cause pain.[6]

Keyboards can be remapped or may be switched between Dvorak and Qwerty layout. USB plugs make it easy to switch between Mac and PC operating systems. Split keyboards are available that allow the user to choose the angle between the halves of the keyboard. The angle between the right and left halves of the keyboard may be adjustable, or the entire keyboard may split in half to vary the distance between the halves depending on user need. The two halves may be adjusted in the shape of a tent (tented keyboards) to follow the natural angle of the forearms while typing.[7] Lateral tilt may also be set by the user. The lateral tilt tends to reduce stress on the forearms. Some include optional padded palm supports and armrests. Fixed split keyboards have standard keyboard spacing but vary the keyboard angle for more natural finger accommodation. Sculpted keyboards follow the natural shape of the hands and length of the fingers so less motion is required to depress the keys.

Some learning is required for all of these keyboards. According to a study, 65 percent of people who acquired alternative keyboards bought them for relief.[8] According to this survey, many preferred the split, curved keyboard layout with wrist rests for reduced pain while typing. In all, 81 percent of respondents stated that an alternative keyboard was better than a standard keyboard.[9] In a NIOSH study, however, it was determined that test subjects found no difference in user comfort whether an ordinary keyboard or several alternative type split keyboards were used.[10]

Consider whether the ergonomic keyboards can fit into the available desk space and whether they are compatible with computer hardware and software already in place and if alternative input devices will work with the system. Those keyboards that have depressed surfaces for the keys (like wells) might make it difficult for the user to see the keys if he or she is not a touch typist. Alternative keyboards must be fitted to the individual user because needs are so different. In the Wright study it was found that there are basically two major groups of keyboards that are desired—the fixed split keyboards that are commercially marketed and the specialized keyboards that are offered in medical equipment catalogs, like the sculpted and adjustable angle keyboards that cost a lot more. There is no single solution. There is no guarantee that a specific keyboard will work or that it will not even cause more stress-related pain.

For people who depend on alternative mice for computer input, an on-screen keyboard may be the answer. HandsOFF is an on-screen keyboard that works with switches and speech output and other functions can be performed by keystrokes (http://www.zygo-usa.com).

FrogPad single-hand keypads allow full keyboard use with one hand. These are also handy for use with PDAs that have very small keys and are difficult for people without mobility problems to use (http://www .frogpad.com).

ALTERNATIVE AND EXPANDED KEYBOARDS

MALTRON carries a variety of adaptive keyboards for special needs. MALTRON also carries single-hand keyboards, single fingerboards, and mouthstick-adapted computer entry for those people with print disabilities and motor impairments (http://www.maltron.com).

Expanded self-contained keyboards with large letters that give auditory feedback are designed for people with severe motor disabilities (http:// www.ekegelectronics.com/).

The expanded keyboard from MALTRON is a solidly constructed keyboard that can be wiped clean. It may be used with toes as well as fingers. Numbers can double as mouse keys and Togglemouse software (included) allows for easier access. It has color-coded keys for function—black on white for letters and numbers, black on pink for F-keys, and keys on yellow background for control keys.

L-Type ergonomic keyboard: this keyboard has a central group of keys and can be used by either right or left hand. Keys are at an angle to minimize downward movement of the fingers. Space keys and other frequently used keys are set for thumb keying, reducing many keystrokes, and hand rests allow for relaxing of hands and fingers between typing.

MALTRON carries keyboards designed for one finger use or a mouthstick. The keyboard itself may be placed on a movable arm and set in different positions for the user. There are different language layouts for English, UK and U.S., French, German, Swedish, Norwegian, and Spanish. Prices for ergonomic keyboards range from 275 British Pounds to 550 British Pounds for an expanded keyboard. The company offers an online training course.

DataHand keyboard—a sculpted keyboard completely separated into halves where each half may be placed where it is most comfortable for the user. No wrist motion or finger extension is required. Keys are operated magnetically and very little force is needed to activate the keys. Fingers are not required to move much while providing full control. www.datahand.com.

Keyboard trays must be considered for a specific keyboard. If there is no room to accommodate the mouse or other input tool, then the user may have to reach a distance and thereby cause shoulder stress and pain.

ALTERNATIVE MICE

There are many alternative mouse options available. Computer input may now be accomplished with almost any part of the body—hand, fist, one finger, foot: eye gaze and head trackers: mechanical or optical touch pads like laptops, trackballs, joysticks similar to those used in games, mouse pens, and glide point.

FOOT-CONTROLLED MICE

Sometimes the addition of foot pedals for computer control may make computer control easier or even possible for those with mobility impairments. STEP-ON-IT is a foot pedal control, available at http://www.bilbo.com/asstech.html.

Foot pedals can augment hand control when more than one key needs to be depressed at a time. They also work with voice recognitions systems. The foot pedal works best when used as a mouse button click tool.

There are many models available. The Footime and No Hands Mouse are two representative mice. For the No Hands one pedal moves the cursor; the other pedal clicks the mouse. The regular hand mouse can be used concurrently with the foot mouse.

One part of the Footime mouse (from Fentek Industries) controls the cursor and the other part of the Footime mouse controls various other clicks. The pedal may be reprogrammed for custom commands (http://www.fentek-ind.com/nh-mouse.htm). Arm supports for those who use a manual mouse and footrests help make this an ergonomically comfortable computer setup.

TRACKBALL MICE

Trackball mice are one of the cheapest and easiest means to make mouse functions available for those with limited mobility in the hands and fingers or for those who need to reduce shoulder movement. The trackball consists of a stationary unit with a ball attached. The ball is moved with one finger to move the cursor and mouse clicks are accomplished with the thumb for left click and a finger for right click. Trackballs come in many designs that fit the hand and are available cordless. They also require very little desk room for movement.

HEAD TRACKING DEVICES

Head tracking devices are available for people with no hand mobility or spasticity. These devices work on infrared technology for detection and a transmitter worn on the head translates head or eye movements into computer input signals. SmartNav 4AT is a head tracker from EnableMart. The unit requires very little actual head motion. It allows typing on a virtual keyboard on the computer.

HeadMouse Extreme is another head tracking device that translates even very small head motions into cursor movements on the computer and allows typing with an on-screen keyboard. It is available from EnableMart. The sensor may be placed on eyeglasses or on the forehead of the user.

QuadJoy-Sip-n-Puff mouth mouse. This is a fast or slow sip-and-puff mouthstick system for four-button and scroll movement. The pointer speed is adjustable. It does not require much energy to operate (http://www.quadjoy.com/quadjoy.htm).

TetraMouse—http://tetramouse.com/features.html—is a unique hands-free mouse that may be activated by tongue, hand, or foot. It plugs into the USB port and has optional software for virtual keyboard use. It is compatible and functional with other mice and is capable of precision input like photo editing.

3M Ergonomic Mouse (from MALTRON) looks like a joystick but must be moved around on the surface to function. It is designed to make it easier to grip. Keys are built into the mouse.

The BigTrack is a single large button excellent for people who have limited motor control. A touch with hand or fist will click the mouse. The BigTrack works with a USB port.

Cirque Smart Cat Touchpad. Hot links can be programmed in for single touch operation for various functions. Mouse clicks are performed by touch on the touch pad (http://www.cirque.com/pages/?section=3&page=31).

Touch pad technology allows precise cursor movement and eliminates stress on wrist, elbows, and shoulders by keeping the hand in a stationary position.

IntelliKeys by IntelliTools is a membrane keyboard that has a choice of six different overlays for Macintosh or Windows computers. The overlays vary in keyboard configuration and high-contrast colors. The function and area of the keys can be changed to provide several larger keys. There are keyguards available separately for those with limited motor function (Available from NanoPac, Inc.: http://www.nanopac.com/IntelliKeys.htm).

One of the easiest ways to adapt the mouse for those with print disabilities is to make use of the features in the Windows XP or Vista program and using the built-in on-screen keyboard. The screen is also navigable by using the arrow keys. Other alternative input devices are trackball mice and joysticks, switch and button control, head tracking devices or eye pointing devices, or even the newest brain-wave input. Another easy way to access computer function is by voice-activation, also built-in feature of the Windows XP or Vista. www.microsft.com/enable.

For people with severe mobility limitations, a large, easily operated device called the BIG Baby Button (http://www.rjcooper.com) may be of value, or the Super-Switch from RJ Cooper, a five-inch switch for mouse clicks and other applications.

SOFTWARE

OPERA: This is a web browser for those with varying disabilities to facilitate web browsing with a single key. The mouse may be operated with simple gestures. The browser may be voice-controlled and web pages navigated when a microphone is added to the computer. The browser works well for people who need alternative input devices. Opera also functions as a screen reader. Tutorials may be found on www.opera.com.

Morseall is a free program for Linux computers that enables people with mobility problems to use Morse code on their computer. People who can control up to three switches may use the program (http://morseall.org/). Microsoft has a comprehensive web site for all of their assistive technology (www.microsoft.com/enable).

TUTORIAL FOR MOBILITY DISABILITIES
WINDOWS XP AND VISTA

A simple aid for reducing typing is the Auto-correct feature in Microsoft Word program. It allows short letter sequences to type standard text like an address. Auto correct settings allow repeated long words to be typed automatically and quickly.

The easiest way to access help for mobility or dexterity problems is through the Wizard in Windows XP.

Start–All Programs–Accessories–Accessibility Wizard. Click "next" until a screen appears asking for help in specific topics.

Click the box.

Click "next."

The next screen enables the Stickykeys option. Stickykeys enable the user to press one key at a time for functions that require keys to be pressed simultaneously like cont-alt-del. The correct option to press would be "yes."

The next option is Bounce Keys. It enables the user to allow the computer to ignore repeated keystrokes and is especially useful for those with hand tremors.

The following screen enables a slider with choice of speed for ignored keystrokes and a blank line to practice keystrokes to find an acceptable setting for Bounce Keys. It can be set to beep aurally when it accepts a keystroke.

Toggle Keys sound when Caps Lock, Num Lock, or Scroll Lock is pressed.

There is also help available in the form of a keyboard. The arrow keys may be used to perform mouse functions and allow use of the numeric keypad instead of the regular mouse.

There is an option of choosing pointer speed and key functions.

The next screen choice is pointer size and color.

Mouse button settings and mouse speed are also options.

The last page lists the changes that have been made and allows a choice to keep the changes or to undo them.

On-Screen Keyboard

The on-screen keyboard is accessed through Start-All Programs-Accessories-Accessibility-On-Screen Keyboard.

The on-screen keyboard is small but is useful with the screen magnifier. The "keyboard" setting on the keyboard allows choice of enhanced or standard keyboard and regular or block letter layout, and a choice of the number of keys.

Enhanced keyboard contains the number panel.

"Settings" under "keyboard" allows sound, font choice, and type options.

"Typing" mode under "settings" permits choice of click, hover, or joystick to select letters.

The UTILITY MANAGER (From All Programs)

Then Click Accessories Accessibility Utility Manager to show whether the on-screen narrator and magnification are running. This is useful because it allows the user to choose assistive technology options.

Ease of Access Center—Vista offers options for those with mobility impairments.

"Use the computer without a mouse or Keyboard"—This option allows keyboard bypass and enables alternative input devices to be used on the on-screen keyboard. Joysticks or other tracking devices may be used.

The next option, "Avoid using the mouse and keyboard," allows speech recognition to be set up.

"Make the mouse easier to use" enables settings and adjustments of available pointers in Vista or compatible pointers from other sources.

"Make the mouse easier to use" option enables settings of the mouse similar to Windows XP: size and colors of the pointers may be set here.

"Make the mouse easier to use" enables settings and adjustments of available pointers in Vista or compatible pointers from other sources.

Controlling the mouse with the keyboard: Click on the option "turn on mouse keys" and then "set up mouse keys," which will bring up keyboard shortcuts and pointer speed.

"Make the keyboard easier to use" enables setting up of mouse, sticky, toggle, and filter keys.

This field also allows adding of a Dvorak keyboard and changing keyboard settings, character repeat rate, and blink rates of the cursor.

SPEECH AND DICTATION

Under Ease of Access Center=Speech recognition.

Or under Speech recognition in the control panel.

Either of these options pulls up the menu for setting up speech recognition on Windows Vista.

Connect microphone to the computer. Microphone and volume are adjusted first.

In the next option, a command reference sheet is offered of what to say to the computer to follow certain commands. For instance, say "click recycle bin" and the computer will follow the command.

From this point, you will be able to use voice commands for the computer. However, it is recommended that the interactive tutorial be used to train the computer to better recognize words and speech patterns of the user. This is a fairly sophisticated speech recognition system. The user may immediately start using voice commands to navigate through the menus with simple commands. It will take some training, however, for the computer to take dictation.

WEB RESOURCES

Assistive Technology Vendors—http://www.nettietatpconsultants.com/atvendors
.html
DOIT—http://www.washington.edu/doit/Brochures/DRR/mobility.html#L1. List of
web sites related to mobility disorders. A group of web sites related to mobility
impairments and issues.
Mobility Index—http://www.icdri.org/Mobility/index.htm. Resource list for people
with mobility disabilities.
Assistive Technology and 508 Compliance—http://www.at508.com/links.cfm.
Comprehensive list of technology resources for all kinds of impairments for
section 508 compliance.
DOIT Video—http://www.washington.edu/doit/Video/wt_mobility.html; free video
for people with mobility impairments.
Audio cassettes—http://freeclassicaudiobooks.com/. web site for free audio books
ready for downloading.
LIST OF MOUSE PRODUCTS—http://us.geocities.com/tim_hobbs.geo/mousetrp.htm
SPEECH SYSTEMS—http://us.geocities.com/tim_hobbs.geo/s_rec1.htm. A list of
voice-activated systems.
AT Vendors—http://atto.buffalo.edu/registered/Resources/ATProductVendors.php.
Comprehensive list of vendors for disability products—http://www.mobility
-health.com/directory/Disability_Resources.html
Web site for mobility impairments organized by states and subject—http://
www.latan.org/atDevices.shtml; list of resources for variable assistive
technology.
Don Johnston—http://www.donjohnston.com
Penny & Giles—http://www.pgcontrols.com
TASH—http://www.tashinc.com
Web site for free audio books ready for downloading—http://freeclassic
audiobooks.com/
Adjustable keyboard article—http://www.tifaq.org/articles/alternative_keyboard
_survey-feb98-scott_wright.html
NIOSH Home Page on the World Wide Web—http://www.cdc.gov/niosh/
homepage.html
DHHS (NIOSH) Publication No. 97–148—http://www.cdc.gov/niosh/homepage
.html
Request a free copy of bibliography of alternative keyboard research and information
on how to implement ergonomic equipment for the workplace.

MOBILITY RESOURCES

Hardware

Many vendors offer 30-day trials or will come to your site to demonstrate their
product. Products are Microsoft compatible.
AbleTrack Trackball Mouse (MAB Assistive Technologies)—http://www
.mabatech.com/

AirLink Cordless Switch (AbleNet, Inc.)—http://www.donjohnston.com/products/
access_solutions/hardware/airlink_cordless_switch/index.html

Avant Prime Programmable Keyboard (Creative Vision Technologies, Inc.)—http://
www.cvtinc.com/products/keyboards/prime.htm

BASS Switches (Don Johnston, Incorporated)—http://www.ilcaustralia.org/home/
search4.asp?state=QLD&page=21&MC=62&MinC=24

BAT Keyboard (Infogrip, Inc.)—http://www.google.com/search?q=BAT+Keyboard
&rls=com.microsoft:en-us:IE-SearchBox&ie=UTF-8&oe=UTF-8&sourceid
=ie7&rlz=1I7GGLL_en

Battery Device Adapter (AbleNet, Inc.)—http://www.enablemart.com/Battery
-Device-Adapter

BIG Step-by-Step Communicator (AbleNet, Inc.)—http://www.enablemart.com/
Big-Step-by-Step-Communicator

Bite-or-Puff (Med Labs, Inc.)—http://www.medlabsinc.com/Med_Labs/BITE-OR
-PUFF.html

Cirque Easy Cat, Cirque Smart Cat, Smart Cat PRO (Cirque Corp.)—http://
www.cirque.com/

Click-N-Type—http://www.lakefolks.org/cnt/

Compact Keyboard and Guard (Inclusive TLC)—http://www.inclusivetlc.com/Products
/ViewProduct.aspx?psid=96

CRUISE adapted track pad (AbleNet, Inc.)—http://www.mobilityville.com/ablenet
-cruise_adapted_trackpad

Cutepdf Writer—http://www.cutepdf.com/products/cutepdf/writer.asp

Cyberlink Brainfingers Hands Free Controller (Brain Actuated Technologies)—
http://www.brainfingers.com/

Darci USB Morse (WesTest Engineering Corp.)—http://assisttech.info/equipment/
eq_mice.htm

Don Johnston Switch Interface Pro (Don Johnston, Incorporated)—http://
www.donjohnston.com/products/access_solutions/hardware/switch_interface
_pro_5/index.html

Dual Switch Latch and Timer (AbleNet, Inc.)—http://www.infogrip.com/product
_view.asp?RecordNumber=681

DynaVox co-pilot (DynaVox Technologies)—http://www.dynavoxtech.com/
products/copilot/

DynaWrite (DynaVox Technologies)—http://www.dynavoxtech.com/products/
dynawrite/

eeZee Mouse CURSOR (LaZee Tek)—http://www.lazeetek.com/html/eezee
_cursor.html

eeZee Mouse PRO (LaZee Tek)—http://www.lazeetek.com/html/eezee_pro.html

eeZee Mouse SWITCH (LaZee Tek)—http://www.marblesoft.com/products.php
?activity=30

Enlarged/Reduced Keyboards with Infrared Remote Control (ZYGO)—http://
www.zygo-usa.com/flexi.html

ErgoClick (Attain)—http://www.ergoclick.com/

Eyegaze Edge Communication System (LC Technologies/Eyegaze Systems)—http://
www.eyegaze.com/content/assistive-technology

EyeMax (DynaVox Technologies)—http://www.dynavoxtech.com/products/eyemax/

EZ Call (Med Labs, Inc.)—http://www.medlabsinc.com/Med_Labs/E-Z_CALL.html

Flexiboard (ZYGO Industries, Inc.)—http://www.zygo-usa.com/flexi.html

Freedom Extreme (Words+, Inc.)—http://www.words-plus.com/web site/products/syst/f2k_extreme_tb.htm

Freedom Toughbook (Words+, Inc.)—http://www.gokeytech.com/freedom_tough-book_communication_devices.htm

Gus! Communicator PCs (Gus Communications, Inc.)—http://shop.gusinc.com/main.sc;jsessionid=9622B42399B1713016FF8D0C680654BA.qscstrfrnt02

Gus! Mouse/Switch Interface (Gus Communications, Inc.)—http://www.axistive.com/the-gus-mouse.html

HeadMouse Extreme (Origin Instruments Corp.)—http://www.orin.com/access/headmouse/

IntelliKeys USB (Cambium Learning Technologies)—http://www.synapseadaptive.com/intellitools/new/IntelliKeys_USB.html

IndeMouse (Adaptive Computer Control Technologies)—http://www.acctinc.ca/?articleID=3

IntelliSwitch (Madentec Limited)—http://www.madentec.com/products/intelliswitch.php

Jouse2(Compusult Limited)—http://www.jouse.com/

JoyBoard (Compusult Limited)—http://www.hear-it.com/h_joyboard.html

Joystick SAM (RJ Cooper and Associates)—http://www.rjcooper.com/sam-joystick/index.html

Keyguards (Turning Point Therapy and Technology, Inc.)—http://www.turningpointtechnology.com/

KinderBoard (Chester Creek)—http://www.chestercreek.com/KinderBoard.html

Kinesis Contoured Ergonomic Keyboard (Kinesis Corp.)—http://www.thehumansolution.com/kierpr.html?gclid=COLn3bG0kaICFYpM2godb-gi5cQ

Kinesis Maxim Split-Adjustable Keyboard (Kinesis Corp.)—http://www.kinesis-ergo.com/max-spec.htm

Kinesis Savant Elite Programmable Foot Switch (Kinesis Corp.)—http://www.kinesis-ergo.com/fs-savant-elite.htm

LaZee Mouse Cursor (LaZee Tek)—http://www.lazeetek.com/html/lazee_cursor.html

LaZee Mouse Pro (LaZee Tek)—http://www.lazeetek.com/html/lazee_pro.html

LaZee Mouse Switch (LaZee Tek)—http://www.lazeetek.com/html/lazee_switch.html

Let-Me-Type—http://www.clasohm.com/lmt/en/

LinkSwitch (Adaptivation, Inc.)—http://www.adaptivation.com/Adaptivation_web site/Adaptivation_ECUs.html

Lipsynch (Adaptive Computer Control Technologies)—http://www.acctinc.ca/

LongView (Avocent Corp.)—http://www.avocent.com/assets/0/2319/2343/2465/2466/e4e4da23-8991-4bc9-b11a-4ab322126903.pdf

MACAW-5 (ZYGO Industries, Inc.)—http://www.briserv.com/zygo/new/product.cfm?id=3

Magic Touch Add-On Kit (KEYTEC, Inc.)—http://www.magictouch.com/KTMT-2400W.pdf

Magic Wand Keyboard (In Touch Systems)—http://www.enablemart.com/Catalog/Alternative-Keyboards/Magic-Wand-Keyboard?gclid=CLWUtre4kaICFRmf-nAodOSgBjg

Magi-Mouse (Magitek, LLC)—http://www.usatechguide.org/getsinglecompany.php
?thecompanyid=727&vmode=1

MALTRON Ergonomic Keyboard L-Type (Applied Learning Maltron USA)—http://
www.maltron.com/maltron-kbd-dual.html

Mercury II (Tobii ATI)—http://www.tobiiati.com/corporate/products/past
_products.aspx

Merlit Interactive Learning Station (InfoCor)—http://www.mysatalight.com/
markets/index.asp

MiniMerc (Tobii AT)—http://www.tobiiati.com/corporate/products/past_products/
minimerc.aspx

Mini Relax (*AbleNet, Inc.*)—http://www.enablemart.com/Mini-Relax

Mini Relax with X-10 (AbleNet, Inc.)—http://www.disabledonline.com/products/
direct-products/switches/timers-and-controls/mini-relax-with-x10-package/

Mini-SwitchPort (P. I. Engineering, Inc.)—http://www.rjcooper.com/mini-switch
port/index.html

Multimedia Max Complete System (Multimedia Designs, Inc.)—http://www.multi
mediadesigns.com/

MyTobii P10 (Tobii ATI)—http://www.tobii.com/assistive_technology/products/
mytobii_p10.aspx

Natural Reader—http://www.naturalreaders.com/?gclid=CNb-gau8kaICFR2Y2
AodXGURjg

NoHands Mouse (Hunter Digital, Ltd.)—http://www.footmouse.com/

100 Percent Touch less Keyboard (Special Needs Computers)—http://
www.specialneedscomputers.ca/index.php?l=product_detail&p=127

Optimist-3HD (ZYGO Industries, Inc.)—http://www.zygo-usa.com/optimist
3hd.html

Point It (AbleNet, Inc.)—http://www.ablenetinc.com/AssistiveTechnology/tabid/55/
Default.aspx

Polyana-4 with Persona (ZYGO Industries, Inc.)—http://www.zygo-usa.com/polyana4
.html

PowerLink 4 Control Unit (AbleNet, Inc.)—http://www.ablenetinc.com/Assistive
-Technology/EnvironmentalControlUnitsECU/PowerLink4controlunit/tabid/
500/Default.aspx

Progress (ZYGO Industries, Inc.)—http://www.zygo-usa.com/progress.html

QuadJoy Mouse (Street Electric Mfg Co.)—http://www.quadjoy.com/

Quick Glance 3 eye tracker (EyeTech Digital Systems, Inc.)—http://www.inition
.co.uk/inition/product.php?URL_=product_mocaptrack_eyetech_quickglance3
&SubCatID_=22

QuickStart Communication Kit (AbleNet, Inc.)—http://www.google.com/products
?q=QuickStart+Communication+Kit+(AbleNet&rls=com.microsoft:en-us:IE
-SearchBox&oe=UTF-8&rlz=1I7GGLL_en&um=1&ie=UTF-8&ei=G74O
-TOrmGYWglAfXvIht&sa=X&oi=product_result_group&ct=title&resnum
=3&ved=0CCwQrQQwAg

R.A.T. (Rodent Activated by Touch) (Adaptivation, Inc.)—http://www.adaptivation
.com/Adaptivation_Web site/Adaptivation_ECUs.html

Relax 3 with the Tash Telephone (AbleNet, Inc.)—http://store.ablenetinc.com/item
_detail.aspx?ItemCode=83100

Rock adapted joystick (AbleNet, Inc.)—https://www.ablenetinc.com/computeraccess/

SAJE Communicator (SAJE Technology)—http://www.saje-tech.com/telephone.html

Sicare Standard and Light II (AbleNet, Inc.)—http://www.ablenetinc.com/Assistive
-Technology/EnvironmentalControlUnitsECU/SiCareProducts/tabid/453/
Default.aspx

Single Switch Latch and Timer (AbleNet, Inc.)—http://www.ablenetinc.com/
Support/ProductPhotos/tabid/401/Default.aspx

SmartNav AT (RJ Cooper and Associates)—http://www.thehumansolution.com/
smnavhafrmop.html?gclid=CL7ulYHBkaICFROdnAodkiUUjg

Snap Switch Caps (AbleNet, Inc.)—http://www.ablenetinc.com/Support/Product
-Photos/tabid/401/Default.aspx

Specs Switch (AbleNet, Inc.)—http://www.google.com/search?q=Specs+Switch&rls
=com.microsoft:en-us:IE-SearchBox&ie=UTF-8&oe=UTF-8&sourceid=ie7&rlz
=1I7GGLL_en

SS-Access PC Package (Academic Software, Inc.)—http://www.acsw.com/

Switch Accessible Trackball (Lekotek of Georgia, Inc.)—http://www.lekotekga.org/
tbspecs.htm

Switch Adapted Mouse (Infogrip)—http://www.infogrip.com/product_view.asp
?RecordNumber=88

Switch Interface Pro 6.0 (Don Johnston, Incorporated)—http://www.donjohnston
.com/products/access_solutions/hardware/switch_interface_pro_5/index.html

Switches (ZYGO)—http://www.zygo-usa.com/toolstrd.html

Swifty (Origin Instruments Corp.)—http://www.orin.com/access/swifty/

TASH Joystick (AbleNet, Inc.)—http://www.ablenetinc.com/Store/Tash+Joystick/
tabid/205/Default.aspx?ItemCode=25020

Tech/Scan (Advanced Multimedia Devices, Inc.)—http://www.spectronicsinoz.com/
product/techscan-8-plus

Tech/Speak with Environmental Controls (Advanced Multimedia Devices)—http://
www.acciinc.com/Test/test/Speech_Generating_Devices/techspeak.htm

Tech/Talk with Environmental Controls (Advanced Multimedia Devices)—http://
www.amdi.net/

Tellus Mobi (Jabbla)—http://www.jabbla.com/software/products.asp?Lid=5
&pnav=;2;&item=16

Tellus 3+ (Jabbla)—http://www.tfeinc.com/shop/index.php?_a=viewProd&productId
=2627

TetraMouse (TetraLite Products)—http://www.tetralite.com/mouse/

U-Switch (Compusult Limited)—http://www.hear-it.com/uswitch_2switch_v8
_110106.pdf

USB Keyboards (AbleNet, Inc.)—http://www.ablenetinc.com/Support/Product
Photos/tabid/401/Default.aspx

USB Switch Interface (QuizWorks Company)—http://quizworks.com/usb_switch
_interfaceplus.html

Viewport, Computer Video Adapter (P. I. Engineering, Inc.)—http://www2.
shopping.com/xPO-P-I-Engineering-PI-Engineering-Viewport-trade-Computer
-Video-Adapter-for-USB

VisionBoard2 (Chester Creek)—http://www.google.com/products?q=VisionBoard2
+(Chester+Creek)&rls=com.microsoft:en-us:IE-SearchBox&oe=UTF-8&rlz=1I7
GGLL_en&um=1&ie=UTF-8&ei=JskOTNbpDpDS8QT_p5imCw&sa=X&oi
=product_result_group&ct=title&resnum=1&ved=0CCUQr-QQwAA

Voice Tracker USB (Acoustic Magic, Inc.)—http://www.activeforever.com/p-2276
    -acoustic-magic-voice-tracker-array-microphone.aspx?CMPID=G_Hearing
    Loss_VoiceTrackerMicrophone_Voice%20tracker%20USB&gclid=CJa0xo
    HKkaICFQPJsgodg1wMjg

Wave switch-adapted trackball (AbleNet, Inc.)—http://store.ablenetinc.com/item
    _detail.aspx?ItemCode=20030300

Wave wireless switch-adapted trackball (AbleNet, Inc.)—http://store.ablenetinc.com
    /item_detail.aspx?ItemCode=20030400&showRating=1

Wireless Switch Interface (QuizWorks Company)—http://quizworks.com/
    wireless_switch_interface.html

Woodpecker (Jabbla)—http://www.jabla.com/software/products.asp?Lid=4&pnav
    =;2;&item=10

X-Keys Desktop and Professional PS/2 and USB (P. I. Engineering, Inc.)—http://
    www.xkeys.com/xkeys.php

X-Keys Footpedal USB & PS/2 (P. I. Engineering, Inc.)—http://www.xkeys.com/
    xkeys/xkfoot.php

X-Keys Stick USB & PS/2 (P. I. Engineering, Inc.)—http://www.xkeys.com/xkeys/
    xkstick.php

X-Keys USB Matrix Board (P. I. Engineering, Inc.)—http://www.xkeys.com/custom/
    xkmatrix.php

Y-mouse PS/2 to USB Adapter (P. I. Engineering, Inc.)—http://www.xkeys.com/
    ymouse/whym08.php

Y-key key Dual Keyboard Adapter PS/2 (P. I. Engineering, Inc.)—http://
    www.xkeys.com/ymouse/whym04.php

Y-mouse PS/2 Dual Mouse Adapter (P. I. Engineering, Inc.)—http://
    www.amazon.com/PI-Engineering-Y-Mouse-Splitter-Pointing/dp/
    B0000510T2

Y-see two (P. I. Engineering, Inc.)—http://www.xkeys.com/ymouse/whym06.php

ZoomText Large-Print Keyboard (Ai Squared)—http://www.aisquared.com/images/
    uploads/ZTLargePrintKeyboard.pdf

SOFTWARE

Boardmaker (Mayer-Johnson, LLC)—http://www.mayer-johnson.com/default.aspx

Cintex4 (NanoPac, Inc.)—http://www.nanopac.com/Cintex4.htm

CoWriter SE (Don Johnston, Incorporated)—http://www.donjohnston.com/down
    -loads/topic_dictionaries/tdsereadme.html

CubeWriter (MK Technologies)—http://www.marblesoft.com/products.php?sub
    -group=16

Discover:Setups (Madentec Limited)—http://www.madentec.com/downloads/tutorials/
    8_managing_setups.pdf

DiscoverScreen (Madentec Limited)—http://www.infogrip.com/product_view.asp
    ?RecordNumber=186

Dr. Peet's TalkWriter (Interest-Driven Learning, Inc.)—http://www.drpeet.com/

Dragger32 AutoClick Utility (Origin Instruments Corp.)—http://www.orin.com/
    access/dragger/index.htm

Dragon NaturallySpeaking Preferred (Nuance Communications, Inc.)—http://
    www.nuance.com/naturallyspeaking/

Eurovocs Suite (Jabbla)—http://www.jabbla.com/software/products.asp?Lid=4&pnav
=;2;&item=10

Eye-cons, Version 2.0 (KidAccess, Inc.)—http://www.kidaccess.com/html/products/
cd/main.html

EZ Keys (Words+, Inc.)—http://www.words-plus.com/website/products/soft/
ezkeys.htm

Five Finger Typist (SoftDawn Software)—http://www.typeonehand.com/

Gus! Dwell Cursor (Gus Communications, Inc.)—http://www.synapseadaptive.com/
augcom/gus/Cursor.htm

Gus! Scanning Cursor (Gus Communications, Inc.)—http://www.gusinc.com

Gus! Talking Calculator (Gus Communications, Inc.)—http://www.synapse
adaptive.com/augcom/gus/Multimedia.htm

Gus! Word Prediction (Gus Communications, Inc.)—http://www.enablemart.com/
Catalog/Gus-Communications-Inc

Lekotek Shareware (Lekotek of Georgia, Inc.)—http://www.lekotekga.org/
product.htm

No-Keys (Leithauser Research)—http://leithauserresearch.com/nokeys.html

Onscreen with WordComplete (Innovation Management Group, Inc.)—http://
www.imgpresents.com/

Overlay Maker 3 (Cambium Learning Technologies)—http://www.adaptivetr.com/
educational/intellitools/overlay-maker-3

ScreenDoors (Madentec Limited)—http://www.madentec.com/intro/

NOTES

1. Forrester Research, Inc., "Findings about Working Age Adults," 2003, Updated February 14, 2008. http://www.microsoft.com/enable/research/phase1.aspx (May 2, 2009).

2. Bureau of Labor Statistics quoted by Carol and Richard Eustice, "What is Carpal Tunnel Syndrome," http://www.about.com/od/carpal/g/tunnelsyndrome/htm, June 16, 2006 (May 1, 2009).

3. "Working Together: Computers and People with Mobility Impairments," DO-IT, Disabilities, Opportunities, Internetworking, and Technology, University of Washington, March 21, 2008, http://www.washington.edu/doit/Brochures/Technology/wtmob.html (May 3, 2009).

4. Tank, Elsebeth and Frederiksen, Carsten. "The DAISY standard: entering the global virtual library," in *Library Trends*, March 27, 2007.

5. Manaris, Bill and Harkreader, Alan. "Suitekeys, a Speech Understanding interface for the Motor Controlled Challenged," in *Proceedings of the Third International ACM SIGCAPH Conference on Assistive Technologies*, www.cs.colc.edu, April 15–17, 1998, 108–115.

6. "Computer Keyboard Design," CUErgo-Cornell University ergonomics web site, http://ergo.human.cornell.edu/AHTutorials/ckd.htm (accessed May 2, 2009).

7. "Computer Keyboard Design."

8. Kenneth Scott Wright and Dr. Anthony D. Andre, "Alternative Keyboards, a User Survey," www.tifaq.org/articles/alternative_keyboard_survey, 1997 (April 4, 2009).

9. Wright and Andre.

10. "Niosh exploratory study on keyboard design finds no Difference in User comfort," www.systoc.com/newscomments/news/february97/keyboard.htm, Publication No. 97–148 (April 4, 2009).

CHAPTER 4

Hearing Impairments

Hearing problems are a major consideration when planning library assistive technology services. Hearing problems may range from minor hearing loss to total deafness. Assistive technology can be as simple as turning up the volume on the telephone or as complicated as having surgical implants.

Libraries may consider assistive technologies for individuals with hearing disabilities that are available through companies like AT&T. People with hearing disabilities usually need to confer with librarians through TTY units and may depend on the many special services provided by telephone companies.

People with hearing disabilities tend to be grouped into a single category when in reality people who have acquired hearing loss during their lifetime or are born deaf may require different assistive technologies. People who are born deaf and use sign language often have difficulty reading because grammar of sign language is often significantly different from that of written and spoken language.[1] Assistive technology may be helpful depending on whether hearing loss develops after speech and language centers of the brain have developed.

Libraries need communications devices for all ranges of hearing disabilities: collections of captioned materials, hearing assist devices, amplified phones, and visible emergency systems. Materials of special interest for the deaf are also a must. According to statistics from SHHH (National Self Help for Hard of Hearing People), 28 million of the 52 million people with a disability have some degree of hearing loss and 2 million of these people are deaf. One third of individuals over 65 are affected by hearing loss.[2]

According to the National Center for Health Statistics 4.5 million people use assistive technology for hearing out of an estimated 34 million with hearing loss. This includes amplified phones, hearing aids, and closed captioning.[3]

The increase in the aging population has a corresponding increase in people with hearing loss. When hearing loss occurs due to aging, often the high-frequency sounds are the first to become difficult to hear. The aging population is at high risk, not only for hearing loss but for concomitant vision loss, mobility problems, and possibly cognitive problems. Disabilities in addition to hearing loss make it especially difficult to address hearing loss in the older population. As the population ages, there will be more and more need for hearing experts to work for older adults to improve quality of life.[4] According to the Centers for Disease Control (CDC) there are approximately 1.7 million people who have some dual sensory loss involving vision and hearing and up to 21 percent of people older than age 70 who have dual sensory loss.[5]

DEGREES OF HEARING LOSS

Normal hearing is the ability to hear 0–20 dB. Mild hearing loss is the ability to hear 20–40 dB with some of the information unavailable to the brain. Mild hearing loss presents some problems distinguishing speech patterns. Moderate hearing loss is the ability to hear 40–55 dB with the ability to hear normal face-to-face conversation. Normal face-to-face conversation may be difficult and will involve some lip-reading. Severe hearing loss is 70–90 dB, with normal conversation being impossible. Conductive hearing loss is the least serious of hearing loss and is caused by damage to the outer or middle part of the ear.

If the hair cells are affected, or there is neurological damage to the ear (sensorineural hearing loss), hearing aids will probably not work because sound can be amplified but the ability to distinguish speech patterns is compromised. A mixed hearing loss is a combination of conductive and sensory motor loss.[6]

Noise-induced hearing loss is caused by damage to the hair cells of the ear that convert sound into electrical stimuli to be interpreted by the brain as sound. Excessive levels of ambient noise may damage these hair cells permanently. Damaging sounds may be one-time events like sonic booms or long-term exposure to lower level sounds. A consistently loud environment is especially dangerous and can cause hearing loss.

It is estimated that 25 percent of workers in the United States are consistently exposed to noise levels that can cause hearing damage. Listening to music at top volume over extended periods of time is especially damaging to the ear (http://www.nidcd.nih.gov/health/hearing/noise.as). Sounds like gunshots can emit damaging sound in the 120–150 dB range. Sounds above 85 dB of long-term exposure can cause permanent hearing loss. It is estimated that about 15 percent of people in the United States aged 20–69 years have permanent hearing loss.[7]

ASSISTIVE TECHNOLOGIES AVAILABLE
FOR HEARING LOSS

Closed Captioning

Closed captioning is the display of printed text on a screen from the verbal dialogue that is occurring in the movie, making it possible for deaf or hard of hearing people to follow the dialogue in a movie. Closed captioning has other applications. It facilitates the learning of foreign languages by providing subtitles. (The term subtitles is used only for foreign languages and assumes the viewer is able to hear.) It is estimated that the greatest number of subtitle users are people who are learning a new language. Closed captioning enables people to follow a movie or news broadcast while in a noisy public environment. The option is available for people who need captions to activate them in their TVs (closed captions) or the captions remain visible on the screen for everyone (open captions). Captions may also be permanently affixed to a movie. These are called "burned-in" captions. Captioning is not visible on HDTV even though it is sent by the broadcaster. The originator of the broadcast must provide a special overlay in order for the viewer to see it.

CLOSED CAPTION DECODERS. These decoders are available to screen out content not suitable for children. V-Gis decoder is available from Harris Communications.

Amplification is a linear process whereby all components of a sound are made louder without separating the desired part of the sound, like speech. Background noise is amplified to the same degree, often making understanding of amplified sound difficult.

Voice processing removes background noise from speech and changes the actual waveforms of speech to make them clearer by a non-linear process and only the desired portions of the sound are amplified.

Loop Telecoil Systems

TELECOILS, t-switches or t-coils, are cores with wire coils around them, or common magnets. A variable magnetic field induces a small electric current in the coil. It differs from an amplified sound from a microphone in that the hearing aid picks up a magnetic signal, which is translated into sound a person hears. Some modern phones are capable of generating magnetic signals that a telecoil can pick up, making it a hearing-aid compatible phone. The ability to read magnetic signals in the absence of a normal microphone allows the reduction of peripheral sound in noisy places and the amplification of only the desired sound.

NECKLOOPS allow a person who needs hearing assistance to hear without using a headset. A neckloop is a miniature loop system worn around the neck and the sound goes directly to the telecoil of the hearing aid instead of a headset. People who do not use t-coils in their hearing aids can use an induction receiver with headphones with the hearing aid on the t-position. Loop systems work best with a directional microphone.

FM Systems

FM systems are a good option for public places that cover a large area. The FM system is built into the microphone of the speaker and the person who needs hearing assistance uses an FM receiver provided for the occasion, his hearing aid and/or neck loop. The systems are given a discrete frequency by the Federal Communication Commission (FCC).

Infrared Systems

Infrared systems work well in large areas where non-portable amplification can be used to advantage. Infrared systems transmit sound by means of infrared light. These are the systems often used in homes to aid a person with hearing loss to listen to the home TV at his desired level.

Induction Loops

Induction loops—for large rooms or individual use. A permanent wire is installed in an inconspicuous place. The sound going through the microphone creates a current in the wire, which generates an electromagnetic field. A hearing aid turned on to the t-coil setting picks up this energy as amplified sound. An induction loop receiver (OW 10) is available from Harris Communications.

Relay Services through Telephone Companies

Telephone companies often provide services and assistive technologies for individuals with hearing loss. Libraries especially must be aware of these services and be prepared to give this information to patrons.

Relay Call Services AT & T (http://relayservices.AT&T.com/support/tips/tty_tips.php). This web site is a good introduction as to what services are available for hearing assistance.

TTY RELAY (http://relayservices.AT&T.com/support/tips/tty_tips.php). The person using a TTY relay service may set up a profile for preferred use with the relay company, enabling the assistant handling the call to know exactly what the user prefers. This saves time and effort each time a person makes a call.

IP CALLS (also called VoIP calls) (http://relayservices.AT&T.com/support/tips/ip_tips.php). IP allows telephone calls through personal computers. A hearing impaired person may use relay service with a communications assistant from the relay company. It combines local phone service and Internet service.

Skype is a free download that allows free phone calls to be made using the Internet. Skype phones enable users to make calls while away from the computer using Skype service. It works with P2P technology (peer-to-peer) and millions of people may use this service simultaneously. Available from skype.com.

VRS SERVICE (VIDEO RELAY SERVICE) This service allows people who are hard of hearing or deaf to use a sign language interpreter and communicate by phone with hearing persons. A video device connects broadband computer and video relay service. It is used for several manual communications systems besides American Sign Language (ASL). This service has been available since 1995 (http://relayservices.AT&T.com/support/tips/vrs_tips.php).

Emergency Relay Phones

VCO phones are voice carry-over phones(http://relayservices.AT&T.com/services/e911/e911_registration.php).

VCO telephones enable a person to speak on the handset and read the response on a screen, allowing persons who are very hard of hearing to communicate with their voice with hearing persons. VCO allows either voice or text at one time so that the VCO user cannot hear the voice if he or she is reading the message. A toll-free relay service relays the call. VCO phones are available from Marilyn Electronics, Rapaport Communications, Inc. The phone can be adjusted up to 30 dB and is hearing aid t-coil compatible (http://www.marilynelectronics.net/products/amplified-telephones/dialogue_vco.htm).

PRIVACY HCO ensures that the translator will stop listening to the conversation for privacy if desired typed translation can be turned on again when the translator sees the typed message.

HCO is "hearing carryover" that allows persons with speech disabilities but normal hearing to hear the person on the telephone. The speech-disabled person then types the message to a relay card that is read to the caller.

VCO-TTY—Voice Carryover to Teletype: The TTY should be set on Baudot mode.

HCO-TTY—Hearing Carryover to Teletype.

BASIC VCO, TWO LINE VCO, and BASIC HCO are also available from telephone companies.

PAY PER CALL—dial 711 or any 800 AT&T relay service.

Telebraille

Telebraille allows people who are both deaf and vision impaired to communicate with people using regular telephones. A telebraille unit connects to a regular telephone. Calls may be placed through a 711 relay or other relay depending on the State.

The Americo VCO phone amplifies up to 26 dB with a loud ringtone and large buttons for people who also have vision problems. These are available from FactoryOutletstore.com.

There are many kinds of hearing-aid compatible phones with large buttons for vision/hearing disabled and a whole range of different phones for varying degrees of hearing loss up to the Braille TTY phones are available for the deaf–blind. There are also assistive wireless FM listening systems including TV listening systems.

Pocketalker

Pocketalker is an amplifier that amplifies sound near the listener, thereby reducing unwanted peripheral sounds. This unit can work with a neckloop by amplifying hearing aids equipped with t-coils. They are available from DSI Company (http://www.notestation.com/tty_wspktd1no1.htm).

Captioned Telephones

Captioned telephones, or captioned relay phones (or Cap-Tel), are valuable for people who have some hearing but sometimes need help deciphering meaning. The phones work in real time so that the person using the phone can see the message in writing as it is being spoken. The Cap-Tel feature may be turned off or on depending on who is using the phone. Many states will give these phones for free to those who need them. Contact the state's Telecommunications Devices Access Program for information. CAP-Tel service is available in most states and is free to all federal employees.

Captioning and HDTV

There is a problem with the new HDTVs and captioning. Captioning is not visible on HDTV even though it is sent by the broadcaster. The originator of the broadcast must provide a special overlay in order for the viewer to see it.

ADAPTIVE DEVICES

There are many adaptive and assistive devices for the hearing impaired. There is visual redundancy on computers; the deaf may use sign language interpreters in school or at work; text telephones and relay systems are now commonplace; there are also signaling systems; e-mail and videoconferencing allow a great deal of advancement for the hearing impaired.

Hearing and TTY Machines

A hearing-aid compatible phone might be a first simple step for a library to provide information access for the hearing impaired. There are inductively coupled hearing-aid phones available for both corded and cordless phones.

TTYs

TTYs or text telephones, formerly often called TDD (telecommunications devices for the deaf), are special telephones that convert spoken words into readable text. They are useful not only for hearing impairments but for people with speech disabilities. The TTY is connected to a regular telephone and a message is typed on the unit's keyboard, enabling the sender and the receiver who must both be using a TTY to see written text. Alternatively a telecommunications relay service may be used whereby someone who does not have a TTY can communicate with a hard of hearing person by talking to the person at the relay service who will type the message to the person using the TTY. The operator then can speak any reply that comes from the TTY.

TTY PRODUCTS

Non-Printing TTYs

Mimicom 4 TTY.UTI-MC4 is a good basic TTY unit with a 20 character display and rechargeable batteries. It is available from Harris Communications (http://www.harriscomm.com/).

The Supercom 440 TTY UTI—SC440 has several more features but costs more. It can be connected directly to a phone line, has 32K memory, two phone jacks, a connector for a printer, and a flashing notification signal for incoming calls.

There are compact TTYs available that are convenient for travel and are compatible with some cell phones. One of these is the Compact/C TTY UTI-COMP-CELL. If the person receiving the call needs a TTY and this is announced by the compact TTY. The convenience here is that the keyboard is full size making it useful for people with finger mobility problems. A list of compatible cell phones is available from Harris Communications at http://www.harriscomm.com/catalog/product_info.php?cPath=41_205&products_id=17090.

Printing TTYs

Printing TTYs are a bit more expensive, but make up for it in convenience. The Miniprint 225 TTY is available from Harris Communications with tone or pulse dialing, 20-character display, flashing light signal, and good signal reception.

The term hearing impaired encompasses both those groups who are totally deaf and those who have reduced hearing. Assistive technology for these two groups varies. Those who have some hearing may prefer to use hearing assistive technology to increase volume and those who are totally deaf will need visual cues for their information. There are several options for visual redundancy in Windows XP, Vista, and Windows 7 that provide visual cues along with or instead of sound.

Hearing-aid coupled system headsets are a good option for a library. The hearing aid must have a t-coil (telecoil) switch to work. The headset is put next to the hearing aid if it is an over the ear set, or over the hearing aid if it is an inner ear hearing aid. The t-coil is switched on and connected to the phone. The signal travels to the earpiece to amplify the sound and the amplified sound goes through the coupler to the hearing aid.

Video Relay Services

For those who prefer to communicate with ASL, video relay service is available. A video conference system is used to relay a hearing impaired person's sign language to a sign language interpreter. The interpreter speaks the message and relays the reply back in sign language.

ASSISTIVE LISTENING DEVICES—TELEPHONE AMPLIFICATION SYSTEMS

Assistive listening devices are amplifier systems (transmitter/receiver) that may be connected to a personal hearing aid, connected to head phones, neckloops, or even work with cochlear implants that may require use of a patch cord. (A neckloop enables FM signal output to connect directly to a hearing aid.) Their function is to increase signal to noise ratio for those people needing hearing assistance. The microphone is placed as close as possible to the source of the sound, so that the listener hears more source sound and less background noise. Telephone amplification systems also make sound easier to hear for non-hearing impaired people. Telephone amplifiers may attach to a phone. Some are portable like detachable amplifiers with volume control that fit over the handset unit and may be carried along to use on public phones. Amplifier handsets attach to a regular telephone unit and amplify the incoming voice. A line amplifier on the other hand amplifies the incoming voice but connects between the handset and the telephone unit. The loudness of the ring of the phone is adjustable for those with hearing problems. A ring amplifier inserted between the phone jack and the phone can increase the ring tone to an acceptable level.

Textnet Service

It is now possible to obtain service over the Internet for TTY users via Textnet from the Hitec Group. Until this software became available, hearing impaired persons needed a phone line for their TTY devices. Now only software and an Internet connection is required and the recipient of the call does not need any special equipment. TTY users do not need Textnet service. There is a set-up fee and reasonable monthly fee for libraries. Total costs differ but are usually more reasonable if there is a library consortium using the same service. The TTY qualifies for E-Rate Priority One as a communications device. It is accessible with user ID and password. More information is available at www.hitec.com and www.textnet.net Phone HITEC 1–630–327–3558.

ASSISTIVE LISTENING DEVICES

Pocket Listenor Assistive Listening Device HCP-Listenor. This device works with t-coil-equipped hearing aids to amplify sound clearly. It also has a connector cable for MP3 players, computers, and radio. It is available from Harris Communications.

WINDOWS XP AND VISTA TUTORIALS

Complete Microsoft tutorials are available at www.microsoft.com/enable.

People with a hearing disability require a visual equivalent of auditory output. Microsoft Windows XP and Vista have a number of built-in devices for people with hearing disabilities. The easiest solution is simply turning up the sound of the computer. A number of other visual equivalents are available.

On Windows XP, click on the amplifier icon on the lower right-hand corner. It has a slider that turns the volume up to the desired level.

The SoundSentry is available through the Accessibility Wizard.

Go to Accessories-Accessibility-Accessibility Wizard.

Click "next" until the screen appears that says "I am deaf or have difficulty hearing sounds from the computer." SoundSentry generates a visual warning instead of an aural one for those who are hard of hearing.

The next option is to display captions if they are available in the user's application.

The next option is in the Control Panel Accessibility symbol.

Click on Control Panel-Accessibility options.

Under the "Sound" tab, the SoundSentry appears that will offer visual warnings instead of the usual sound and gives a choice of the location of the warning—window, caption bar, or desktop.

The next choice is for ShowSounds, which enables captioning if the program is caption capable.

Next on the Control Panel is the Sound and Audio symbol.

The first tab allows changes in computer volume and speaker volume.

The next tab, sound schemes, allows sounds for many different events for the computer. A choice of sound is available. For instance, instead of a beep, you can choose a different sound like a ding. There are many choices available here.

The following tab, "Audio," gives a choice of sound, microphone (recording), and music playback sound volumes.

The "voice" tab has voice recording and voice playback options.

"Notification" permits sound cues or visual cues when accessibility features have been activated.

Text-to-Speech will allow reading aloud of commands. It helps some hard of hearing people to see and hear together for better understanding.

VISTA TUTORIAL/HEARING

Go to the Ease of Access Center: Programs-Accessories-Ease of Access Center.

Or go to Control Panel-Ease of Access Center that brings up the identical above screen.

Click on Use text or visual alternatives for sounds—Sound Sentry.

Click on "save" when the desired notification has been chosen.

Here also visual warnings may be chosen instead of sounds. The active window, the caption bar, or the desktop may be allowed to flash for Attention.

Captions may be activated here.

There is a list of possible sound schemes under the Audio Devices and Sound Schemes where sounds and sound systems may be changed possible for better hearing.

HEARING RESOURCES

American Sign Language—http://www.aslaccess.org/
Article on hearing loss and resources—http://www.ed.uiuc.edu/wp/access/
    hearing.html
Comprehensive list of resources for hearing loss—http://www.abledata.com/
    abledata.cfm?pageid=113573&top=13436&ksectionid=19326
http://teachingtechnology.suite101.com/article.cfm/technology_for_hearing
    _impaired
Large web site with resources for hearing disabilities—http://www.ibwebs.com/
    hearing.htm#basic

Products for deaf. TTY—http://www.blvd.com/assistive_technology_disability
.htm

Resource products for hearing loss—http://www.weitbrecht.com/

AudiTech is a source for hearing products for telephones (voice/TTY) (800) 229–8293,
or write to: Devices and Services for hearing impaired:

Sammons Preston
P.O. Box 5071
Bolingbrook, IL 60440-5071

HARC Mercantile, Ltd.
Hearing Aid Center of Kalamazoo
P.O. Box 3055
Kalamazoo, MI 49003

Project Link
Center for Assistive Technology
University at Buffalo
515 Kimball Tower
Buffalo, NY 14214 (voice/TTY/TDD) (800) 628–2281. Help for people who need
assistive technologies

AudiTech, Inc.
381 Cockrell Road
Vicksburg, MS 39180-0381

CAPTIONING RESOURCES

Gallaudet Media Resources:
Gallaudet University Library
800 Florida Avenue, N.E.
Washington, D.C. 20002-3625
202–651–5051 voice
202–651–5052 TDD

Harris Communications:
6541 City West Parkway
Eden Prairie, MN 55344-3248
1–800–825–6758

National Captioning Institute
5203 Leesburg Pike
Falls Church, VA 22041
1–703–998–2400 voice/TDD

Services and Captioned Material for Hearing Disabled
5000 Park Street North
St. Petersburg, FL 33709
1–800–237–6213 voice/TDD

Sign Media
Burtonsville Commerce Center
4020 Blackburn Lane
Burtonsville, MD 20866
1–877–399–7446

TJ Publishers, Inc.
817 Silver Springs #206
Silver Springs, MD 20910
1–800–999–1168

The Caption Center
125 Western Avenue
Boston, MA 02134
1–617–492–9225

OTHER RESOURCES

Hardware

BoardSpeaker T1200 (Afforda Speech)—http://www.affordaspeech.com/T1200.htm
Closed Caption Display Units (Compusult Limited)—www.CaptionDisplay.com
EZ Call (Med Labs, Inc.)—http://www.zapconnect.com/products/index.cfm/fuse
    -action/products_display_detail/eregnum/2026803/owner_operator_number/
    2026803/product_code/ILP/2026803.html
Gus! Wallet Speaker (Gus Communications, Inc.)—http://www.enablemart.com/
    Gus-Pocket-Communicator
IntelliSwitch (Madentec Limited)—http://www.madentec.com
Interpretype Communicator C1.1 (Interpretype)—http://www.harriscomm.com/
    index.php/equipment/ttys/interpretype.html
Keyguards (Turning Point Therapy and Technology, Inc.)—http://www.turning
    -pointtechnology.com/
LEO (Tobii ATI)—http://www.tobiiati.com/corporate/training/guides_tips_and
    _tricks/leo.aspx
Mercury II (Tobii ATI)—http://www.assistivetech.com/corporate/products/past
    _products/merc.aspx
PA-1 Portable Alarm (Med Labs, Inc.)—http://www.medlabsinc.com/Med_Labs/PA-1
    _ALARM.html
Partner Plus Four (Advanced Multimedia Devices, Inc.)—http://www.amdi.net/pdfs/
    Partner-Plus-Instructions.pdf

Switch Accessible Trackball (Lekotek of Georgia, Inc.)—http://www.lekotekga.org/tbspecs.htm

Switch Adapted Mouse (Lekotek of Georgia, Inc.)—http://www.lekotekga.org/tbspecs.htm

X-Keys USB Switch Interface (P. I. Engineering, Inc.)—http://www.xkeys.com/xkeys/xkswi.php

ZEN (Gennum)—http://www.pocket-lint.com/review/829/zen-gennum-bluetooth-headset-wireless

Software

CaptionMaker Realtime Closed Captioning Software (CPC—Computer Prompting Captioning Co.)—http://www.cpcweb.com/cpc-500/

Dr. Peet's TalkWriter (Interest-Driven Learning, Inc.)—http://www.drpeet.com/interest_driven_learning_article.html

iCommunicator (PPRDirect)—http://icommunicator.com/

Network Telephony Services (NTS) (NexTalk, Inc.)—http://www.nxicom.com/about_us.html

NexTalk VM (NXi Communications, Inc.)—http://nextalk.com/

Other Assistive Technology

Adapt-a-Lap Book Holder (Adapt-a-Lap, Inc.)—http://classic.backbenimble.com/new/pages/adaptalap/index.htm

Adaptive Device Locator System (ADLS) (Academic Software, Inc.)—http://www.acsw.com/

Assistive Technology Tutorial Collection (Atomic Learning)—http://www.atomiclearning.com/k12/en/assistivetechnology?from_legacy=1

Attainment Tabletop Carrel (Attainment Company, Inc.)—http://www.attainmentcompany.com/product.php?productid=16358&cat=0&page=10

Bilingual Picture Symbol Communication Resource (Academic Communication Associates)—http://www.acadcom.com/scripts/prodView.asp?idproduct=875

Book of Picture Symbols for Everyday Communication (Academic Communication Associates, Inc.)—http://www.acadcom.com/acanews1/anmviewer.asp?a=6&z=3

Buddy (Bill & Bud, Inc.)—http://playabilitytoys.com/

Captioning/CART (Alternative Communication Services, LLC)—http://www.acscaptions.com/index.asp

Classroom Audio Technology (Lightspeed Technologies, Inc.)—http://www.light-speed-tek.com/?AspxAutoDetectCookieSupport=1

Closed Captioning Service (CPC—Computer Prompting Captioning Co.)—http://www.cpcweb.com/

Compact/C TTY (Ultratec, Inc.)—https://secure.healthproductsforyou.com/products/Telecommunication-Devices-TDDTTY/3B01/Ultratec-Compact-C-TTY.html

Freedom Machines DVD Education Package (Richard Cox Productions)—http://www.freedommachines.com/pdf%20versions/release12-05-2005.pdf

iDictate Telephone Dictation Service (iDictate.com)—http://idictate.com/

Invisible Clock (Attainment Company, Inc.)—http://www.mobilityville.com/
attainment-invisible_clock

Let's Sign: 4 Seasons eBook (Co-Sign Communications)—www.DeafBooks.co.uk

Let's Sign 5 Little Men in a Flying Saucer (Co-Sign Communications)—
www.DeafBooks.co.uk

Minicom IV TTY (Ultratec, Inc.)—http://www.healthproductsforyou.com/products/
Telecommunication-Devices-TDDTTY/3AFC/Ultratec-Minicom-IV-TTY
.html

News-2-You (News-2-You)—http://www.sedl.org/cgi-bin/mysql/afterschool/
technology.cgi?resource=16

Picture Symbol Language Activity Book (Academic Communication Associates)—
http://www.acadcom.com/acanews1/anmviewer.asp?a=6&z=3

Picture Symbol Stories for Special Learners (Academic Communication Associates)—
http://www.acadcom.com/scripts/prodView.asp?idproduct=874

See It and Sign It—Introduction to ASL (Bill & Bud, Inc.)—http://www.toy
directory.com/monthly/hgg/manufacturer.asp?id=1434&cat=129

Superprint 4425 TTY (Ultratec, Inc.)—http://www.ultratec.com/ttys/printing/
. superprint.php

Superprint Pro80 (Ultratec, Inc.)—http://www.weitbrecht.com/ultratec-superprint
-pro80.html

Toobaloo (Learning Loft, Inc.)—http://www.toobaloo.com/

HEARING RESOURCES

Hardware

Closed Caption Display Units (Compusult Limited)—www.CaptionDisplay.com

Gus! Wallet Speaker (Gus Communications, Inc.)—http://www.enablemart.com/
Gus-Pocket-Communicator

IntelliSwitch (Madentec Limited)—http://www.madentec.com/products/intelli
-switch.php

Interpretype Communicator C1.1 (Interpretype)—http://www.affordaspeech.com/
T1200.htm

Keyguards (Turning Point Therapy and Technology, Inc.)—http://www
.turningpointtechnology.com/KG/KGMGMain.asp

LEO (Tobii ATI)—http://www.tobiiati.com/corporate/training/guides_tips_and
_tricks/leo.aspx

Mercury II (Tobii ATI)—http://www.assistivetech.com/corporate/products/past
_products/merc.aspx

MiniMerc SGD (Tobii ATI)—http://www.assistivetech.com/corporate/products/
past_products/minimerc_sgd.aspx

Partner Plus Four (Advanced Multimedia Devices, Inc.)—http://www.amdi.net/pdfs/
Partner-Plus-Instructions.pdf

Switch Adapted Mouse (Lekotek of Georgia, Inc.)—http://www.lekotekga.org/
tbspecs.htm

Switch Accessible Trackball (Lekotek of Georgia, Inc.)—http://www.lekotekga.org/
   tbspecs.htm
X-Keys USB Switch Interface (P. I. Engineering, Inc.)—http://www.xkeys.com/xkeys/
   xkswi.php
ZEN (Gennum)—http://www.nxzen.com/headsets/nx6000_1.php

Software

CaptionMaker Realtime Closed Captioning Software (CPC—Computer Prompting
   Captioning Co.)—http://www.cpcweb.com/products/product_summary.htm
Dr. Peet's TalkWriter (Interest-Driven Learning, Inc.)—http://www.drpeet.com/
iCommunicator (PPRDirect)—http://www.icommunicator.com/downloads/
   iCommunicator-UserGuide-v40.pdf
Network Telephony Services (NTS) (NexTalk, Inc.)—http://www.nxicom.com/
   about_us.html
NexTalk VM (NXi Communications, Inc.)—http://tap.gallaudet.edu/Standards/ivr/
   NXi/VM.asp

NOTES

    1. John Michael Day, ed., "Guidelines for Library Services for Deaf People," 2nd
Edition, IFLA Professional Reports nr 62, 2000, page10, www.ifla.org/VII/s9/nd1/iflapr-62
.pdf. IFLA Headquarters, the Hague (accessed February 25, 2009).
    2. Huntington, Barbara & Swanson, Coral. "Speech and Hearing." Adults with
Special Needs: A Resource and Planning Guide for Wisconsin's Public Libraries. Wisconsin
State Department of Public Instruction. Division for Libraries, Technology, and Community
Learning-Public Library Development. Madison, WI. Institute of Education Sciences,
Department of Education, Washington. 61–76. 2002. ED482241. http://www.eric.ed.gov
(November 2002).
    3. Jon Schull's weblog, "Disabilities/Impairments," www.cdc.gov/nchs/fastats/
disable.htm. December 18, 2002 (accessed May 8, 2009).
    4. Patricia Krikos, PhD, "Hearing Assistive Technology Considerations for Older
Individuals With Dual Sensory Loss," *Trends in Amplification*, 11, (2007): 273–279.
http://tia.sagepub.com/cgi/content/refs/. DOI: 10.1177/108471304363 (accessed
February 25, 2009).
    5. Gabrielle Saunders, PhD, "An Overview of Dual Sensory Impairment in Older
Adults: Perspectives for Rehabilitation," *Trends in Amplification*, 11, (2007): 243–258.
http://tia.sagepub.com/cgi/content/refs/ (accessed April 20, 2009).
    6. "Speech and Hearing," Ch. 7 (accessed May 7, 2009).
    7. Suter, A. H. and H. E. von Gierke. "Noise and public policy." *Ear Hear*, 8(4) 1987,
188–91, quoted by Timothy C. Hain, MD. "Noise Induced Hearing Loss and Noise
Induced Vestibular Disturbances," http://www.dizziness-and-balance.com/disorders/
hearing/noise.htm (accessed May 10, 2009).

CHAPTER 5

Speech Disabilities

Speech disorders are best defined under the broader category of communications disorders, which include problems in articulation ability, problems with the voice or language, stuttering, inability to speak words due to brain injury, or problems with hearing. The abilities to hear, assimilate information into the brain, and speak are closely interconnected communications skills. Some pathway must be used to convey information to the brain to make communication possible. If a person is unable to speak, sign language with the hands (American Sign Language [ASL]), finger spelling, or pictorial representations of thought like pictures a person may point at must be used. In the 1960s, pictures (POS or point of sales devices) were developed to help people communicate on computers and speech synthesizers. This method of communication was later used in the 1980s in fast-food restaurants to show pictures of orders and enabled non-verbal people to obtain jobs. Because of various types of new technologies, people who were unemployable in the past are now part of the workforce.[1]

The term *alternative and augmentative communication* (AAC) has a combined meaning: Augmentative communication is used to describe methods that aid a person to communicate if he or she has difficulty speaking or is not clearly understood by others. These might be aids using the person's own voice and enhancing it in some way or by using a speech translating service of people who are trained in speech problems. Alternative communication relies on non-verbal communication like picture boards, or speech synthesizers. The user must be able to choose an item in some fashion. If he or she has some motor ability, he or she may point to an item using a finger or hand to activate a switch; or he or she may use a head tracking device or an eye tracking device. Other systems like electronic scanners require that the user choose an item from a series of pictures, words, or letters that appear on the communications board. For manual picture boards, a helper may point to various pictures until the user indicates a choice. There are scanners that speak aloud for word selection for people with vision problems.[2]

CAUSES OF SPEECH DISABILITIES

The inability to speak is probably the most neglected of the problems requiring assistive technology. People are unable to speak for a number of reasons. A major cause of inability to speak is deafness. People who are born deaf generally do not learn to speak well enough to communicate by speech. Profoundly deaf persons may learn to speak with therapy but often do not speak clearly enough to communicate without some kind of assistive technology.

Examples of conditions that may cause speech disabilities are brain damage due to stroke, accident, progressive neuromuscular disorders, laryngectomy or removal of the voice box, aphonia or absence of speech capability, multiple sclerosis, or paralysis.

Apraxia is the inability to speak correctly or consistently what a person wants to say. Apraxia may be congenital or acquired through accident, illness, or disease conditions like stroke, tumors, and head injury, where the parts of the brain responsible for speech are damaged. Aphasia is the inability to speak thoughts that the brain has formulated or the inability to understand written or spoken words. It is usually caused by brain injury involving the speech centers of the brain. Newest treatments include drug therapy to be used in conjunction with speech training by a speech pathologist.

Autism is a major cause of inability to communicate verbally, as is ALS (amyotrophic lateral sclerosis) in its later stage. Until recently the key electronic aid for people who have soft voices or difficulty speaking was to increase volume with microphone. Microphones function by either directional preference (relatively cheap) or distance preference (noise canceling), which is more expensive.[3] Noise canceling microphones pick up sounds close to it preferentially and reject noise farther away. This technology has been used for several years in pilots' headsets with great success.

Voice wave technology has been instrumental in improving the communications ability of people who have difficulty speaking. It consists of a microphone, a signal processor, and sound feedback to the speaker.[4]

Alternative and Augmentative Communication

There are many modern hardware and software devices that can help people communicate who are unable to speak. Some devices are as simple as picture boards that the person can point at. Unfortunately, people who cannot speak clearly have problems using dictation systems like Dragon Naturally Speaking and the dictation software in Windows and Vista.

However, by training the computer to an individual voice it may be possible for people with speech problems to use this software.

Methods of AAC

Word Prediction

Pictures of the desired word Alphabet methods may rely on spelling, word prediction, or choosing whole words from a list.

Semantic Compaction Systems (SCS)[5] is a system for software for those needing alternative communication. It is a pictorial language technique software licensed to Prentke-Romich Company using the concept of pictures with multiple meanings and is available for computers, personal digital assistants (PDAs), games, phones, and texting. It is sold under the name of Minspeak. This process makes it possible to use fewer keystrokes with icons in order for people who need alternative communication or who have speech difficulties to send commands to their small-screen computers. It enhances speed and utility for handheld computers. Minspeak is available in English, French, German, and other languages. It is unique because it allows the person using AAC to specify the meaning of a symbol that may have several different meanings. For instance, a symbol of a rainbow could mean rain or happy (http://www.minspeak.com/faq.html).

Minspeak works with computers and portable communications devices like Pathfinder, Vantage, Vanguard, SpringBoard, and ChatBox, which were designed to be used with the Minspeak communications system. Words are based on a simple sequence of pictures that lead to more complicated meanings, with the first icon usually being the subject matter to be discussed and the second icon communicating the intent of the subject. For instance, from a total of 32 icons, several hundred sentences may be formed (http://www.minspeak.com/faq.html).

Software Products

AAC Keys is a mouse and keyboard emulation system for Windows and Macs. AAC Keys enables the computer to translate commands from an alternative AAC system via serial port into keystrokes and mouse input and is used as an alternative to SerialKeys. AAC Keys is available in English and German. It works on Windows 95-XP and Vista and on Mac OS X. AAC Keys is free for the downloading but a donation is requested if possible to AAC (www.aacinstitute.org).

Dasher word prediction: http://www.inference.phy.cam.ac.uk/dasher/Novice.html and http://www.inference.phy.cam.ac.uk/dasher/Dasher Summary2.html. Dasher is a freeware word prediction tool for the speech disabled. Dasher works by offering groups of letters, offering the subsequent statistically more probable letters depending on what letter or letter combinations are chosen first. Dasher learns the writing style of the user and improves on offering the letter groups and words that the user will likely choose. More space is devoted to more likely combinations of letters than unlikely ones. The Dasher web site describes using the word prediction tool like "driving a car." Dasher 4.10.0 has been available since March 2008. Dasher is useful not only for people with speech problems but also for people who have mobility handicaps like using one hand or mouthstick to enter data. It is also a time and effort saver for personal communications devices (http://www.inference.phy.cam.ac.uk/dasher/Demonstrations.html). There are demonstrations available at this web site. Dasher receives support from the Gatsby Foundation and AEGIS (open Accessibility Everywhere: Groundwork, Infrastructure, Standards).

EZ Keys for Windows is a word prediction program. AAC users who are literate much prefer word programs over pictorial and symbol programs. It allows faster communication and the person merely types what he or she wants to say. EZ Keys offers abbreviated word expansion, word prediction, choice of common phrases, voice capability, and screen reader. Input may be through simple typing or an alternative input device like a switch. Abbreviation expansion enables the user to begin typing a word, and then several possible alternatives appear for the person to choose. EZ Keys enables users to create phrases that they commonly use for quick recall. Information is typed on the word processor and the screen reader may be used to speak the message. A variety of input devices may be used, like head trackers, joystick, switches, or Morse code.

If Side talk with Instant Phrases is used with EZ Keys, the user can create messages or use preprogrammed messages, which are grouped by category making communication quick and simple (www.gokeytech.com/e_z _keys.htm).

Talking Screen by Words+ is a communication software for people who prefer to communicate with symbols. The displays are customized for the individual user. The software allows synthesized or digitized speech and can have entire messages tagged to a symbol of choice. Personal photos may also be used for symbols and symbols may be edited for custom use. Any combination of pictures and text is possible and symbols may be sequenced for more complicated meanings. Talking Screen can be accessed with common tools like mouse, joystick, touch screen, or switches (www.words-plus.com/web site/products/soft/talkscrn.htm). It works with Windows 95, 98, ME. Version 3.0 is compatible with Windows XP 2000.

Speaking Dynamically Pro from Mayer Johnson enables a computer to become a communications tool. It is a program for making custom word board with color symbols with a choice of voice output for the symbols. It allows alternative input devices like touch screen or joystick. It requires the use of an additional database, Boardmaker, to customize the communications symbols. It works with Windows 95 up or Macs (http://www.infogrip.com/product_view.asp?RecordNumber=213).

Dynavox system software (DSS) enables communications pages to be made for people with speech or learning disabilities on the computer and transferred to a portable unit like DynaMyte and DynaVox. It is for Windows XP and Macintosh computer systems. DynaVox's (12-inch version) large surface area is useful for people with motor disabilities. DynaMite (the smaller version) is a portable picture/symbol personalized communications device that will speak desired messages (http://www.dynavoxtech.com/products/m3/). The advantage of the DynaVox system is that just one system of communications may be used on several hardware platforms.

DynaVox has a new version of its software as of 2008, version 1.05, to be used with V and Vmax speech output units. Important features are an Eyegaze system for people who can use only their eyes to communicate, an e-book reader, Internet navigation capability, and Bluetooth capability for controlling a different computer. This software is free with devices purchased from DynaVox (http://www.dynavoxtech.com/company/press/release.aspx?id=18).

Gus! Multimedia speech software from Microsoft has five communications system for a wide variety of communications applications. The user may move about pages quickly and has a choice of scanning method—by rows or columns or scanning by auditory means. Gus! has a link to Gus talking keyboard and Gus Easy Talk and offers text-to-speech so the user can communicate with words or by symbols only. It has lists of topics and phrases to choose from or the user may create topics and add them to the lists. It can provide speech from any Windows application.

SpringBoard is a communications device available from Liberator, a Prentke-Roehmich company. SpringBoard Lite is a portable pictorial communications tool. It has a touch screen and is easily programmed. It weighs 1.1 kg, with 8 hours of battery power (http://www.pri-liberator.com/products/springboard-lite.aspx).

Vantage Lite from Liberator is a portable communications tool from PRC. It has more features but is much more expensive than the SpringBoard. It can use picture text, or phrase-based Minspeak programs—WordCore, Unity, as well as non-Minspeak programs. It also has built-in computer and cell phone capability.

SpeechPRO—AAC communications software for Windows or Vista with an on-screen keyboard and symbol displays on the same screen. It is a combination of the Speech System, Talking Keyboard, and Easy Talk. It is Vista compatible. SpeechPro is free with Gus! Communications systems (http://www.gusinc.com/speechsystem.html). It is available in choice of languages and neo-speech male and female voices (http://www.gusinc.com/speechpro.html). It allows customizing of keyboard layouts—changing fonts and colors to make keyboard easier to read. It also allows creating pages of words and linking between symbols with tabs. The system can be made as simple or as complicated as desired.

Hardware Units

ChatPC Silk + Enkidu Palmtop communications device from NanoPac Inc. Technologies is a portable communications device for people with speech disabilities that enables the user to program his own communications symbols if desired. The device comes with 10 different screens (http://www.nanopac.com/Impact%20Palmtop%20Enkidu%20Augmentative%20Comunications%20Device%20AAC.htm).

iChat is an emergency communication system from AAC. It is a simple manual card system with symbols to be used in an emergency in case a computer or a communications device breaks down. It is available in several different languages and culturally preferred skin color in the symbols.

LightWRITERS text-to-speech units, portable, ZYGO industries, Inc. This unit is convenient because it has two faces, one for the user to write on and one for the person being spoken to (http://www.tobii.com/en/assistive-technology/north-america/). Also available is LightWRITER SL/35 BIGKEYS for those with additional visual or motor disability. Keys are arranged alphabetically, so touch-typing is not required.

TuffTalker by Words+ is a portable communications device that provides computer access. It is shock resistant; it has Talking Screen software and touch screen.

Mercury is a Windows XP-based AAC system. Windows software is already installed. It is an ideal communications system with voice (http://www.tobii.com/en/assistive-technology/north-america/).

The Gus! Pocket Communicator is useful for people with speech problems. It requires that the person be able to type words or use pages of words and phrases already on the unit. It is available at http://www.gusinc.com/pocketcomm.html.

SPEECH SERVICES

STS (speech-to-speech) is a service provided through teletype and telephone service. It is a useful technology for those who have problems speaking clearly enough to be understood by most people. A communications assistant trained in speech disorders relays the call directly to the recipient. The service is available throughout the United States, Puerto Rico, and the Virgin Islands.[6]

Hearing carry-over phones: People with a speech disability with hearing may communicate this way. The caller types the message and the other person speaks normally. VCO—voice carry-over phones. These phones are described in previous chapters.

Fluency system: The telephone fluency system uses auditory feedback correction to correct stuttering.

FaceToFace from Freedom Scientific is a personal communications device using the PAC Mate. A deaf–blind person can receive messages in Braille on this unit and respond either with voice or by typing messages on the PAC Mate.

COMMUNICATION DIFFICULTIES—SPEECH AND WRITING DIFFICULTIES

Speech enhancers or speech generating devices (SGDs) work in several different ways or combinations of ways: volume increase and speech synthesis. It takes on the speech characteristics of the user and combines user's speech with synthetic speech for more natural sounding voices. It works on telephone or over speakers and increases inaudible voices to normal volume. Voicewave Technology Inc. is one manufacturer of SGDs.

Communications Devices, Software, and Products for People with Speech Disabilities

Alternative and Augmentative Communications

AAC devices and systems include communication boards, keyboards, speech synthesizers, text-to-speech hardware and software, laser pointers, headwands, mouthsticks, and sign language. AACs also include note takers, word prediction systems, voice amplifiers, artificial larynx, mechanical picture boards, and service like speech phone services and Braille devices and services.

Tobii C8 is a communications device for communication with words or symbols; it is lightweight and portable with a touch screen. Various software programs are available depending on the user's need. It has synthesizer for speech, e-mail capability, and chat capability. It is available from Tobii ATI company (www.assistivetech.com).

Tobii C12 is a speech device with optional eye tracking control, keyboard, mouse control, or switch control (www.assistivetech.com).

TuffTalker Convertible is a communications device that uses a laptop computer. The computer can be switched to a communications device and back to a computer with a simple switch. It comes with Words+ Talking Screen, EZ Keys, or Speaking Dynamically Pro and works with Windows. It offers freedom for people who are unable to communicate by voice (http://www.words-plus.com/website/products/syst/tufftalk_convertible.htm).

AT&T Natural Voices: These voices are composed of real human voices to sound more real than synthetic speech (http://www.words-plus.com/website/products/syst/natural_voices.htm).

ARTIFICIAL LARYNX

Artificial larynx is a small electronic unit that makes speech possible for people who have had laryngectomies. The unit is held against the throat and makes sounds that the user can form into speech. It is an artificial sounding speech and some people are reluctant to use this device.

WINDOWS XP TUTORIAL

Choosing a Voice for Text-to-Speech

Go to START. Select "Control Panel." Make sure the system is in "Classic" view. Classic view may be obtained from the "Appearance" tab on display properties in the Display module in the control panel.
Choose the SPEECH module.
Choose "Speech Properties—Voice Selection."
Choose the voice of choice. Voices can be previewed.
Choose OK.

Voice Speed

The SPEECH module also enables the voice speed. Adjust the slider to the desired speed and choose OK.

Choosing Audio Device for Text-to-Speech Playback

From the Control Panel in "Classic" view:

Choose "Speech."
From the Speech Properties dialogue box choose Audio Output.
Go to text-to-speech Sound Output to Text-to-Speech.
Choose "Use preferred audio output device" or choose a device from list.
After a device is chosen, you may select the sound volume.
Click OK to finish.

SPEECH RECOGNITION FROM OFFICE 2002

Word Processor

Speech Recognition

Go to TOOLS section on Office Program and click on Speech.
Click on the blue bar at the top of the screen TOOLS and click on TRAINING.

A series of passages are offered to read for training the computer to a specific user speech profile. The more the user reads, the better the speech tool will be able to understand the user. Training session begins with proper microphone adjustment.

TUTORIAL WINDOWS VISTA

Even though speech recognition functions require a person to be able to speak, the Vista Speech Recognition Program has a training program so that the computer will be better able to understand the speech input.

Setting up the microphone
Go to Ease of Access Center Speech Recognition
Click on Set up Microphone
From the Microphone Setup Wizard choose your microphone and its
  settings
Finish the instructions for the Setup Wizard.

Start with the Control Panel and choose the Ease of Access Center and click on Speech Recognition. Click on "Train your computer to better understand you." You will be given several passages to read and the more you read to the computer, the better the computer will be able to understand your individual speech characteristics. Choose "More Training" and read the subsequent passages. This training might be sufficient to enable a person who does not speak clearly to use the speech recognition system.

WEB RESOURCES FOR SPEECH PROBLEMS

Rehabilitation Engineering and Assistive Technology Society of North America (RESNA)—http://www.aacinstitute.org/index.html.

AAC Institute is a resource for people with communications disorders. It is a non-profit organization for people who need augmentative or alternative communication. The web site contains practical materials as well as research papers.

ISAAC International Society for Augmentative and Alternative Communication—http://www.isaac-online.org/ie/categories/AAC-Practice/AAC-Overview/.

NIDCDC Toll-free: (800) 241–1044

Toll-free TTY: (800) 241–1055

Address: 1 Communication Avenue, Bethesda, MD 20892-3456

E-mail: nidcdinfo@nidcd.nih.gov

Internet: www.nidcd.nih.gov

Rehabtool.com is a company that offers a wide variety of communications applications, computer access systems, and voice recognition systems.

http://www.speechville.com/
http://www.aacinstitute.org/index.html
http://www.nidcd.nih.gov/. Web site for National institute for deafness and
other communications problems.
http://www.aacinstitute.org/Resources/ProductsandServices/aackeys.html
1000 Killarney Drive
Pittsburgh, PA 15234

Prentke Romich Company
Web site: Prentke Romich Company
Telephone: 330–262–1984; 800–262–1984
E-mail: info@prentrom.com
Address: 1022 Heyl Road
Wooster, OH 44691
Prentke Romich Company is a company that specializes in alternative
communications devices. It offers Liberator, AlphaRalker, DeltaTalker,
and WalkerTalker in the communications category and WiVik and Jouse
for access to computers, and alternative telephones.

Words+
Web site: Words+
Telephone: 800–869–8521; 661–723–6523
E-mail: info@words-plus.com
Address: 1220 W. Avenue J
Lancaster, CA 93534
Words+ is a company specializing in AAC. It offers picture and text
alternate communications for Windows applications.

Electronic Speech Enhancement
Web site: Electronic Speech Enhancement
Telephone: 314–731–1000; 888–463–7353
E-mail: Service@SpeechEnhancer.com
Address: 143 McDonnell Boulevard, Bldg. B
Saint Louis, MO 63042
Speech Enhancer uses electronic systems to clarify speech caused by cerebral
palsy, ALS, laryngectomy, and inaudible voices due to tracheotomy.

SPEECH RESOURCES

Advanced Auditory Communicator (Enabling Devices, Toys for Special Children)—
    http://enablingdevices.com/catalog
Base Trainer (Advanced Multimedia Devices, Inc.)—http://www.trademarkia.com/
    base-trainer-76547985.html
BIGmack Communicator (AbleNet, Inc.)—http://www.ablenetinc.com/Assistive
    -Technology/CommunicationProducts/tabid/56/Default.aspx

Bilingual SpringBoard Lite (Spanish/English) Prentke Romich Company (PRC)—
http://www.prentrom.com/component/option,com_docman/Itemid,1/task,
cat_view/gid,53

Blackhawk (ADAMLAB, LLC)—http://www.adamlab.com/

Bluetooth Wireless Switch Prentke Romich Company (PRC)—http://
www.prentrom.com/press/bluetoothswitch

BoardSpeaker T1200 (Afforda Speech)—http://www.affordaspeech.com/T1200.htm

ChatBox40 (Saltillo Corp.)—http://www.saltillo.com/faq/index.php?cat=10

ChatBox40-XT (Saltillo Corp.)—https://www.saltillo.com/shop/catalog/product
_info.php?cPath=1&products_id=38

ChatBox-DX (Saltillo Corp.)—http://www.saltillo.com/products/index.php
?product=33

ChatBox (Saltillo Corp.)—http://www.saltillo.com/products/index.php?product=33

ChatPC-4 (Saltillo Corp.)—http://www.saltillo.com/products/index.php?product=32

ChatPC-Silk (Saltillo Corp.)—http://www.saltillo.com/

Chipper (Adaptivation, Inc.)—http://www.adaptivation.com/Adaptivation_Website/
Adaptivation_Comm_Aids.html

Communication Builder—http://www.tecsol.com.au/ComBuilder.htm

Desktop LCD Touchmonitors (Elo TouchSystems)—http://www.elotouch.com/
products/lcds/1515l/default.asp

Digicom 2000 (The Great Talking Box Company)—http://www.greattalking
box.com/newjoomla/index.php?option=com_content&view=article&id=7
:stick-to-the-code&catid=1:latest-news

DynaVox co-pilot (DynaVox Technologies)—http://www.dynavoxtech.com/
products/copilot/

DynaWrite (DynaVox Technologies)—http://ca.dynavoxtech.com/products/dynawrite/
features.aspx

e-talk CS 8400 (The Great Talking Box Company)—http://www.greattalking
box.com/

e-talk Tablet w/cradle (The Great Talking Box Company)—http://www.abledata.
com/abledata.cfm?pageid=113582&orgid=113392

EasyTalk (The Great Talking Box Company)—http://www.greattalkingbox.com/
aac-products/easytalk-aac-device.html

ERICA System (*Eye Response Technology*)—http://www.axistive.com/erica
-standard-system.html

Express One (Attainment Company, Inc.)—http://www.attainmentcompany.com/
product.php?productid=16534&cat=316&page=1

EyeMax (*DynaVox Technologies*)—http://www.dynavoxtech.com/company/press/
release/detail.aspx?id=33

EZ Call (Med Labs, Inc.)—http://www.medlabsinc.com/Med_Labs/E-Z_CALL.html

Facilitator (KayPENTAX)—http://www.kayelemetrics.com/index.php?option
=com_publication&Itemid=5&id=16&menu_id=46&subid=195

FL4SH Scanning Communicator (AbleNet, Inc.)—http://www.ablenetinc.com/
SupportDocuments/175.pdf

Freedom Extreme (Words+, Inc.)—http://www.words-plus.com/website/products/
syst/f2k_extreme_tb.htm

Freedom LITE (Words+, Inc.)—http://www.words-plus.com/website/products/syst/
f2kliteP_series.htm

Freedom Toughbook (Words+, Inc.)—http://www.words-plus.com/website/products/syst/f2ktb.htm

Go Talk 4+ (Attainment Company, Inc.)—http://www.attainmentcompany.com/home.php?cat=277

Go Talk 9+ (Attainment Company, Inc.)—http://www.attainmentcompany.com/product.php?productid=16147&cat=337&page=1

Gus! Communicator PCs (Gus Communications, Inc.)—http://www.enablemart.com/Catalog/Gus-Communications-Inc

Gus! Pocket Communicator (Gus Communications, Inc.)—www.gusinc.com

Hawk II, III (ADAMLAB, LLC)—http://www.adamlab.com/Hawk,HawkII,HawkIII.htm

Hearit Lending Library (Hearit Company)—http://www.atohio.org/devices.html

Hearit Perfect (Hearit Company)—http://www.hearitllc.com/

Hearit Personal Listening System (Hearit Company)—http://www.rehabmart.com/category/Personal_Listening_Systems.htm

Hearit SE (Hearit Company)—http://www.hearitllc.com/

IntelliSwitch (Madentec Limited)—http://www.madentec.com/products/intelli-switch.php

Interpretype Communicator C1.1 (Interpretype)—http://www.interpretype.com/

KeyboardCommunicator KC200 (Afforda Speech)—http://www.affordaspeech.com/KC200.htm

Keyguards (Turning Point Therapy and Technology, Inc.)—http://www.turningpointtechnology.com/

Lighthawk (ADAMLAB, LLC)—http://www.adamlab.com/Lighthawk.htm

Lightwriter SL87 and SL88 (DynaVox Technologies)—http://www.toby-churchill.com/files/downloads/LWmanual.pdf

Lingraphica (Lingraphica)—http://www.aphasia.com/patients/index.aspx?gclid=CNmwxtqZlKICFQG3sgod1FolFA

Logan ProxTalker (ProxTalker.com LLC)—http://www.proxtalker.com/

Magic Touch (KEYTEC, Inc.)—http://www.magictouch.com/

Mercury II (Tobii ATI)—http://www.assistivetech.com/corporate/products/past_products/merc.aspx

Merlit Interactive Learning Station (InfoCor)—http://merlit.info/news/050109-%5Blinkedin%5D.asp

MessageMate 40 (Words+, Inc.)—http://www.words-plus.com/website/products/hand/mm.htm

Mini-Message Mate (Words+, Inc.)—http://www.words-plus.com/website/products/hand/mm.htm

MessageMate 20 (Words+, Inc.)—http://www.aactechconnect.com/products/pdf/3.pdf

MiniMerc (Tobii ATI)—http://microscience.on.ca/catalogues/MSC-AAC%20Catalogue.pdf

Multi-Level MessageMate 40 (Words+, Inc.)—http://www.gokeytech.com/multi-level_messagemate_40.htm

Multi-Speech (KayPENTAX)—http://www.kayelemetrics.com/

MyTobii P10 (Tobii ATI)—http://www.assistivetech.com/corporate/products/mytobii_p10.aspx

No Touch Talker (Attainment Company, Inc.)—http://www.attainmentcompany.com/product.php?productid=16154&cat=338&page=1

Optimist-3HD (ZYGO Industries, Inc.)—http://www.zygo-usa.com/optimist3 hd.html

PA-1 Portable Alarm (Med Labs, Inc.)—http://www.abledata.com/abledata.cfm ?pageid=113583&top=0&productid=101319&trail=0

Partner Plus Four (Advanced Multimedia Devices, Inc.)—http://www.amdi.net/pdfs/ Partner-Plus-Instructions.pdf

Partner Plus Stepper (Advanced Multimedia Devices, Inc.)—http://www.amdi.net/ pdfs/Partner-Plus-Stepper-Instructions.pdf

Persona Mobile (ZYGO Industries, Inc.)—http://www.zygo-usa.com/persona _mobile.html

Polyana-4 with Persona (ZYGO Industries, Inc.)—http://www.zygo-usa.com/polyana4 .html

PolyTABLET with Persona (ZYGO Industries, Inc.)—http://www.zygo-usa.com/ persona.html

Put-Em-Arounds (Enabling Devices, Toys for Special Children)—http:// enablingdevices.com/catalog/assistive_technology_devices_used_in _education

Quick Glance 3 eye tracker (EyeTech Digital Systems, Inc.)—http://www.eye techds.com/assistivetech/users/

QuickPAD IR (QuickPad Technology Corp.)—http://multi-speech.software .informer.com/

QuickStart Communication Kit (AbleNet, Inc.)—http://www.ablenetinc.com/ Support/ProductPhotos/tabid/401/Default.aspx

Say-it! SAM Communicator (Words+, Inc.)—http://www.words-plus.com/website/ products/syst/say_it_sam.htm

Say-it! SAM Tablet XP1 (Words+, Inc.)—http://www.words-plus.com/website/ products/syst/sam_xp1.html

Say-it! SAM Tablet SM1 (Words+, Inc.)—http://www.words-plus.com/website/ products/syst/sam_SM1.html

Sequencer (Adaptivation, Inc.)—http://www.adaptivation.com/Adaptivation _Website/Adaptivation_Manuals/SEQ90RAND90%20.pdf

SmartSpeaker SS200 (Afforda Speech)—http://www.affordaspeech.com/SS100.htm

Speech Assistant (JITA Technologies, LLC)—http://www.speechassistant.com/ About_Us.html

Speech Generating Devices (Words+, Inc.)—http://www.aetna.com/cpb/medical/ data/400_499/0437.html

Step-by-Step Communicator with Levels (AbleNet, Inc.)—http://www.ablenetinc .com/

StepPAD (Attainment Company, Inc.)—http://www.attainmentcompany.com/ product.php?productid=16158&cat=339&page=1

Superhawk Six, Superhawk Twelve, and Superhawk Plus (ADAMLAB)—http:// www.adamlab.com/SuperhawkPlus.htm

SuperTalker Progressive Communicator (AbleNet, Inc.)—http://store.ablenetinc. com/item_detail.aspx?ItemCode=10002800

Switch Interface (P. I. Engineering, Inc.)—http://www.xkeys.com/xkeys/xkswi.php

Talara-32 (ZYGO Industries, Inc.)—http://www.zygo-usa.com/talara.html

Talking Symbols Notepad (AbleNet, Inc.)—http://www.ablenetinc.com/Support Documents/170.pdf

Tango (Blink Twice)—http://www.dynavoxtech.com/products/tango/faq.aspx
Tech/Scan (Advanced Multimedia Devices, Inc.)—http://www.trademarkia.com/techscan-76547991.html
Tech/Scan Plus (Advanced Multimedia Devices, Inc.)—http://www.abledata.com/abledata.cfm?pageid=113583&top=0&productid=75658&trail=0
Tech/Speak (Advanced Multimedia Devices, Inc.)—http://www.amdi.net/
Tech/Talk (Advanced Multimedia Devices, Inc.)—http://www.amdi.net/
Tech/Talk with Environmental Controls (Advanced Multimedia Devices.)
Tellus Mobi (Jabbla)—http://www.jabbla.com/images/files/mobi_en.pdf
Tellus Smart 2 (Jabbla)—http://www.novitatech.org.au/product.asp?p=247&id=2756
Tellus 3+ (Jabbla)—http://www.jabbla.com/software/content.asp?Pag=3&pnav=;2
Tobii Devices (Tobii ATI)—http://www.assistivetech.com/corporate/home.aspx
TuffTalker Convertible (Words+ Inc.)—http://www.axistive.com/tufftalker-convertible.html
Vanguard Plus Prentke Romich Company (PRC)—http://support.prentrom.com/category.php?id=6
Visi-Pitch IV (KayPENTAX)—http://www.kayelemetrics.com/index.php?option=com_product&Itemid=3&controller=product&task=learn_more&cid%5B%5D=85
VisionKey Series (H. K. EyeCan, Ltd.)—http://www.eyecan.ca/
VocaFlex (Saltillo Corp.)—http://www.saltillo.com/products/index.php?product=36&product_id=14
VoiceNote mPower (HumanWare)—https://www.humanware.com/en-usa/products/blindness/braillenotes
VoicePal 8 (Adaptivation, Inc.)—http://www.axistive.com/voicepal-8.html
VoicePal 8K (Adaptivation, Inc.)—http://www.adaptivation.com/Adaptivation_Website/Adaptivation_Comm_Aids.html
VoicePod (Attainment Company, Inc.)—http://www.attainmentcompany.com/product.php?productid=16148&cat=316&page=4
X-Keys USB
X-Tender, 24-Volt Dual Channel Power Converter (Bloorview Kids Rehab)—http://www.xtender.com/xtender

OTHER ASSISTIVE TECHNOLOGY

Adapt-a-Lap Book Holder (Adapt-a-Lap, Inc.)—http://www.adaptalap.com/
Adaptive Device Locator System (ADLS) (Academic Software, Inc.)—http://www.acsw.com/
Assistive Technology Tutorial Collection (Atomic Learning)—http://www.atomiclearning.com/k12/en/assistivetechnology
Associates, Inc.—http://www.acadcom.com/acawebsite/prodView.asp?idprod-uct=800
Attainment Tabletop Carrel (Attainment Company, Inc.)—http://www.theradapt.com/store/ShowProduct.aspx?ID=74
Bilingual Picture Symbol Communication Resource (Academic Communication Associates)—http://www.acadcom.com/scripts/prodView.asp?idproduct=875

Book of Picture Symbols for Everyday Communication (Academic Communication
    Buddy (Bill & Bud, Inc.)—http://www.billbuddy.com.au/bb/index.htm
Captioning/CART (Alternative Communication Services, LLC)—http://www
    .acscaptions.com/
Classroom Audio Technology (Lightspeed Technologies, Inc.)—http://www.light
    -speed-tek.com/
Closed Captioning Service (CPC—Computer Prompting Captioning Co.)—http://
    www.cpcweb.com/
Compact/C TTY (Ultratec, Inc.)—http://www.ultratec.com/ttys/portable/
    http://www.ultratec.com/ttys/non-printing/minicom.php
Freedom Machines DVD Education Package (Richard Cox Productions)—http://
    www.adaptiveenvironments.org/neada/site/freedom_machines_new_bilingual
iDictate Telephone Dictation Service—http://www.idictate.com/
Invisible Clock (Attainment Company, Inc.)—http://www.attainmentcompany.com/
    product.php?productid=16160&cat=339&page=1
Let's Sign: 4 Seasons eBook (Co-Sign Communications)—www.DeafBooks.co.uk
Let's Sign 5 Little Men in a Flying Saucer (Co-Sign Communications)—www.Deaf
    Books.co.uk
Picture Symbol Language Activity Book (Academic Communication Associates)—
    http://www.acadcom.com/scripts/prodView.asp?idproduct=836
See It and Sign It—Introduction to ASL (Bill & Bud, Inc.)—http://gifts.
    barnesandnoble.com/Toys-games/See-It-and-Sign-It-Game-Intro-to-ASL/e/
    856259000427
Superprint 4425 TTY (Ultratec, Inc.)—http://www.ultratec.com/ttys/printing/
    superprint.php
Superprint Pro80 (Ultratec, Inc.)—http://www.ultratec.com/ttys/printing/superprint
    -pro80.php
Toobaloo (Learning Loft, Inc.)—http://www.toobaloo.com/

NOTES

1. Rothwell, James and Fuller, Dennis. "Functional Communication for Soft or
Inaudible Voices: A New Paradigm," Annual conference of the Rehabilitation Engineering
and Assistive Technology Society of North America, 2005, www.speechenhancer.com/
docs/RESNAFunctional%20Communication.pdf (accessed May 13, 2009).

2. Pedroddy Bryant Diane and Bryant, Brian R. "Assistive Technology for People with
Disabilities" (Boston: University of Texas at Austin, 2003): 88–89.

3. Rothwell.

4. Rothwell.

5. Semantic Compaction Systems, "Minspeak Software FAQ's," www.minspeak.com/
faq.html, October 10, 2005 (accessed May 12, 2009).

6. "Fact Sheet: Telephone Access for People with Speech Disabilities," ICDRI, 2008.
http://www.icdri.org/News/STS.htm (accessed May 12, 2009).

SECTION III
Accessibility Issues

CHAPTER 6

Providing Accessible Buildings and Learning Spaces

The university library, considered the heart of a university, is a tool for patrons and a gateway for information. This role is accompanied by a responsibility for providing access to resources for all patrons.[1] Accessibility can be best defined as providing a barrier-free environment for everyone.[2]

The Library Services for People with Disabilities Policy (ASCLA, 2009) states that "libraries play a catalytic role in the lives of people with disabilities by facilitating their full participation in society. Libraries should use strategies based upon the principles of universal design to ensure that library policy, resources, and services meet the needs of all people."[3] The top priorities should be to ensure that patrons can get to the physical facility and can navigate the library web site easily.

Some accommodations may involve expensive renovations and high-tech solutions. However, most accommodations are not in fact costly or high tech. Adapting a work table or carrel may be a possibility instead of purchasing furniture that is specifically designed to accommodate wheelchairs. Inexpensive page and screen magnifiers, headphones, page-turning devices, telephone amplifiers, and tape recorders often provide adequate accommodations for individuals with disabilities.

The American Library Association Committee for Accreditation Standards encourages a barrier-free, universal access environment. Standard VI.4 discusses building and facility accessibility. This standard applies to web accessibility as well as to physical access because it specifically states "regardless of form ... of delivery."[4] Standard IV.2 deals with the accessibility of information.

The Americans with Disabilities Act (ADA) states that Title III schools must complete a Facility Self-Appraisal. The principal duty under Title III is to remove existing barriers. Architectural barrier removal is required only if it is "readily achievable." According to the ADA, this means "without much difficulty or expense."[5]

Initially, a transition plan addressing ADA guidelines and other planning areas may be developed by an ad hoc accessibility transition committee. This team should include individuals with disabilities, faculty, library staff, a physical plant person, and field experts. This committee should be involved in discussing any facility alterations.

PHYSICAL ACCESS

Parking for those with a handicapped parking permit should be available in the library parking lot. Handicapped parking spaces should be closely monitored and strict fines enforced for individuals that park illegally. Restrooms should be accessible for patrons in wheelchairs according to the ADA guidelines. If the only elevator is a service elevator, a key should be kept at the circulation desk for individuals with disabilities who need elevator access.

RETRIEVAL OF BOOKS AND JOURNALS

Book and journal retrieval services and procedures should be available for individuals with special needs and these services should have links on library web sites and in print venues. Other special services such as large print copies of articles and books for individuals with visual disabilities should be clearly outlined in the library policy manual. Staff should be aware of these special policies and any forms that are required.

Individual study carrels should be available for quiet study. Spaces should be provided for group study or tutoring.[6]

LISTENING AND VIEWING STATIONS

Individual listening and viewing stations should be available for materials that may be requested from the Library for the Blind & Dyslexic and other sources.[7]

EQUIPMENT

The main issues to consider when purchasing equipment that will meet the needs of individuals with disabilities as well as the needs of all library patrons include:

- Appropriateness of equipment for need or disability;
- Quality of equipment in comparison to similar models;

- Costs—Initial costs, maintenance costs, and costs associated with training;
- Level of training required for training staff and patrons;
- Equalization opportunities.

Postsecondary education programs that receive or benefit from federal funds must "take such steps as are necessary to ensure that no handicapped student is denied the benefits of, excluded from participation in, or otherwise subjected to discrimination because of the absence of educational auxiliary aids for students with impaired sensory, manual or speaking skills."[8] Equipment purchases should involve the input of a committee to provide recommendations for sources of equipment and to secure the necessary funding. Quite often, patrons with disabilities are the best source of information about the most appropriate equipment purchases. They are sometimes knowledgeable about the costs and the level of training required for using assistive devices or equipment.

Proper evaluation of all equipment is crucial for maintaining quality resources for all patrons. Each state has an Office of Rehabilitation Services. This office evaluates assistive equipment and disseminates information on appropriate equipment and funding sources. They provide training for using assistive devices and workshops on assistive technology for libraries and other groups. Some other sources for equipment reviews include the Trace Center at the University of Wisconsin, the Illinois Assistive Technology Project, and The Council for Exceptional Children: Technology & Media Division, and *Closing the Gap* newsletter. Numerous assistive technology companies maintain web sites that provide a good initial source of information.

It is important to evaluate equipment that is already in use to ensure that accommodations can be made to existing equipment so that it will serve the needs of all patrons. For instance, Windows software includes accessibility options. Some of the accessibility options include keyboard options, print and font options, and sound and speech options. This software can be loaded on computers with online public access catalogs and other reference tools in order to make them accessible to patrons with disabilities without having to purchase expensive optical scanning equipment. Larger monitors are recommended for using zoom options.

Large-print keyboards and printers with large-print font should be available. Sound cards, speakers, and headphones would be necessary for sound options.

The main area of concern in most libraries is the online public catalog (OPAC). Some OPACs do not have zoom features for enlarged text or sound programs. Microsoft features described in earlier chapters can be used with most OPACs. A computer interface is available for some systems that have enlarged text and sound enhancements for patrons with disabilities.

Conventional tape recorders should be available for student use. Talking calculators and Library of Congress adapted players may be borrowed for patrons from the Library for the Blind & Dyslexic.

Special adaptive equipment such as accessibility and zoom options that are available on the OPAC, GALILEO, and reference workstations should be noted at the point of reference as well as on the web site. Special equipment may be requested as needed from the Library for the Blind & Dyslexic, Tools for Life, and other sources.

Legal Mandate for Web Design Accessibility

The ADA web site discusses the legal mandates for postsecondary institutions (PL 101-336; PL 105-17). The ADA is not a regulatory law. The ADA addresses important issues such as effective communication, auxiliary aids and services, and discrimination because of a disability.[9] Office of Civil Rights (OCR) complaints and compliance reviews involving Internet access seem to be the most prevalent.

Section 504 of the Rehabilitation Act of 1998 provides guidance to organizations receiving federal funding for making their sites more accessible.

Henderson (2001) gives statistics for each category within the postsecondary education group.[10] These statistics are dated as they are compiled in conjunction with the U.S. census.

Green and Gillespie (2001) discuss a study to determine appropriate technologies and services for individuals with disabilities.[11]

Section 504 of the 1973 Rehabilitation Act is an important milestone for people with disabilities. It is the first civil rights law for people with disabilities because it prohibited federal agencies, public universities, federal contractors, and any other institution or activity receiving federal funds from discriminating based on disability.

The ADA covers accessibility to services, programs, or activities of a public entity for individuals with disabilities.[12] Universal design that would provide services and resources for all patrons is the main thrust in most facilities.

Ingle, Green, and Huprich (2007) discuss making web sites and the Internet accessible and the meaning of the ADA as it applies to these technologies.[13]

Minow and Lipinski (2003) provide an excellent checklist and chapter explaining the various components of the ADA as they relate to digital resources and Internet usage. Another excellent source on this topic is Barbara Mates's (2000) book, *Adaptive Technology for the Internet: Making Electronic Resources Accessible to All*. This book although somewhat dated provides some excellent tips on adapting computer equipment for use with the OPAC and other library equipment and software. Mates focuses on computer adaptations for individuals with visual impairments.

A checklist for library space planning should include the following categories: service areas, collection space, user seating space, staff workstations, meeting room needs special use space, and parking needs.[14] Each of these areas should contain specific guidance for serving individuals with disabilities.

ACCESSIBLE ELEMENTS AND SPACES: SCOPE AND TECHNICAL REQUIREMENTS

The minimum requirements outlined in the *ADA Accessibility Guidelines* are required in new construction and existing facilities unless they are structurally impracticable. The reader should consult the Department of Justice's (July 1, 1994) *ADA Standards for Accessible Design* (revised) for complete information for library building requirements and services.[15]

Americans with Disabilities Act Accessibility Guidelines Checklist for Buildings and Facilities

The ADA checklist has been prepared to assist individuals and entities with rights or duties under Title II, and Title III of the ADA in applying the requirements of the Americans with Disabilities Act Accessibility Guidelines (ADAAG) to buildings and facilities subject to the law. The checklist presents information in summary form on the Department of Transportation (DOT) and the Department of Justice (DOJ) regulations implementing the ADA. This checklist is based on ADAAG as published on July 26, 1991 (sections 1 through 4.35 and special application sections 5 through 9), and September 6, 1991 (section 10). See 56 FR 35408 (July 26, 1991) and 56 FR 45500 (September 6, 1991) as corrected at 57 FR 1393 (January 14, 1992)[16] (http://www.access-board.gov/adaag/checklist/a16.html).

Trotta and Trotta (2001) provide an excellent table with potential solutions for each area on the ADA Checklist. Sannwald (2009) provides checklists for ADA compliance.

Library Name:

Section	Item	Technical Requirements	Comments	Yes	No
8.2	Reading and Study Areas:	Do at least 5 percent (at least one) of fixed seating, tables, or study carrels comply with 4.2 and 4.3.2?			

(Continued)

Section	Item	Technical Requirements	Comments	Yes	No
4.2.4 4.32.2	Seating/ Floor Space:	Do spaces provided for wheelchair users have a 30 x 48 inch clearance?			
4.32.3	Knee Space:	Is the knee space under the table at least 27 inches high, 30 inches wide, and 19 inches deep?			
4.32.4	Height:	Is the top of the table between 28 and 34 inches from the floor?			
4.3.3	Aisles:	Are the aisles leading up to and between the tables or study carrels at least 36 inches wide?			
8.3 7.2(1)	Check-Out Areas:	Is there at least one lane at each check-out area where a portion of the counter is at least 36 inches long and no more than 36 inches high?			

Section	Item	Technical Requirements	Comments	Yes	No
8.3 4.13	Security Gates:	Do security gates or turnstiles comply with 4.13? OR Is there an accessible gate or door next to a turnstile or security device?			
8.4	OPAC and Magazines:	Is the aisle between the OPAC and magazine displays at least 36 inches wide?			
8.5 4.3	Stacks:	Is the minimum clear aisle width between the stacks at least 36 inches? (A minimum clear aisle width of 42 inches is preferred where possible. Shelf height in stack areas is unrestricted.)			

Library Name _____

Library Parking and Drop-Off Areas (ADAAG 4.6)
Are an adequate number of accessible parking spaces available (8 feet wide for car plus 5-foot access aisle)?

Total Spaces
Total spaces—At least one space is accessible and 2 percent of total spaces are accessible.
Total number of accessible spaces:
Are 8-foot-wide spaces, with minimum 8-foot-wide access aisles, and 98 inches of vertical clearance available for lift-equipped vans?

At least one of every eight accessible spaces must be van-accessible (with a minimum of one-van accessible space in all cases).

Number of van-accessible spaces:

Width:

Vertical clearance:

Are the access aisles part of the accessible route to the accessible entrance?
Are the accessible spaces closest to the accessible entrance?

Route of Travel (ADAAG 4.3, 4.4, 4.5, 4.7)
Is there a route of travel that does not require the use of stairs?

Is the route of travel stable, firm, and slip-resistant?

Is the route of travel at least 36 inches wide?

Width:

RESOURCES

Online Resources

Department of Justice—http://www.usdoj.gov/. This site provides links to technical guides, assistance manuals, laws and regulations, Office of Civil Rights complaints, question and answer publications, and design guides.
U.S. Department of Education: National Institute on Disability and Rehabilitation Research web site. This site provides general disability research and information on assistive technologies. Abledata—http://www.abledata.com.

Laws and Regulations

Americans with Disabilities Act. 1990. *U.S.C.* Vol. 42, sec. 12101. Public Law 101-336 The Americans with Disabilities Act of 1990.
Assistive Technology Act. 2004. *U.S.C.* Vol. 29, sec. 3001.

A Guide to Disability Rights Laws—http://www.ada.gov/cguide.htm.
Rehabilitation Act, Section 504. 1973. *U.S. Code Annotated*. Vol. 29, sec. 794.
Rehabilitation Act, Section 508. 1998. *U.S. Code Annotated*. Vol. 29, sec. 794.
Title III Regulation.

Technical Assistance Manuals and Guides

Association of Specialized and Cooperative Library Agencies. 2005. *Revised Standards and Guidelines of Service for the Library of Congress Network of Libraries for the Blind and Physically Handicapped*, Chicago: ALA.
Association of Specialized and Cooperative Library Agencies. 1996. *Revised Standards and Guidelines of Service for the Library of Congress Network of Libraries for the American Deaf Community*, Chicago: ALA.
Department of Justice. ADA Best Practices Tool Kit for State & Local Governments. 2007. http://www.ada.gov/pcatoolkit.htm.
Department of Justice. July 1, 1994. *ADA Standards for Accessible Design* (revised) (http://www.ada.gov/adastd94.pdf).
IMS Global Learning Consortium Inc. 2002. *IMS Guidelines for developing accessible learning applications*. Accessed November 24, 2007. Available at http://ncam.wgbh.org/salt/guidelines/.
Kavenaugh, R. and Skold, B.C. 2005. *Libraries for the Blind in the Information Age: Guidelines for Development*, IFLA Professional Reports No. 86, International Federation of Library Associations and Institutions, available at http://www.ifla.org/VII/s31/pub/Profrep86.pdf.

ADA Information Services

Association on Higher Education and Disability (AHEAD). 2004. *AHEAD: About us*. Accessed November 20, 2007. Available at http://www.ahead.org/index.htm.
Want to Resolve Your ADA Complaint? Consider Mediation—http://www.ada.gov/liblist.htm.

Books

ADA. 1995. *Checklist for existing facilities*. Version 2.1: Adaptive Environments Center.
Berliss, J. R. 1990. *Checklists for implementing accessibility in computer laboratories at colleges and universities* (No. 1.0). University of Wisconsin-Madison Trace Center.
Brinckerhoff, Loring Cowles, Stan F. Shaw, and Joan McGuire. 1993. *Promoting postsecondary education for students with learning disabilities: a handbook for practitioners*. Austin, Texas: Pro-Ed.
Burke, John. 2006. *Neal-Schuman library technology companion: a basic guide for library staff*. New York: Neal-Schuman Publishers.

Deines-Jones, Courtney. 2007. *Improving library services to people with disabilities.* Chandos information professional series. Oxford: Chandos Publishing.

Forrest, M.E.S. 2006. "Toward an Accessible Academic Library: Using the IFLA checklist," *IFLA Journal*, 32(1): 13–18.

Gordon, Michael, and Shelby Keiser. 1998. *Accommodations in higher education under the Americans with Disabilities Act (ADA): a no-nonsense guide for clinicians, educators, administrators, and lawyers.* DeWitt, New York: GSI Publications.

Lazzaro, Joseph J. 2001. *Adaptive technologies for learning & work environments.* Chicago: American Library Association.

Mates, B. 2000. *Adaptive Technology for the Internet: Making Electronic Resources Accessible to All.* Chicago: ALA.

Minow, M. and Lipinski, T. 2003. *The Library's Legal Answer Book.* Chicago: ALA.

Northern College. 2003. *Accessibility checklist.* South Region: Northern College.

Rothstein, Laura F. 1995. *Disability law cases, materials, problems.* Contemporary legal education series. Charlottesville, VA: Michie Butterworth.

Scherer, M.J. 2006. *Institute for matching person & technology, inc.* Retrieved January 9, 2009, from http://members.aol.com/IMPT97/MPT.html.

Trotta, C. and Trotta, M. 2001. *The Librarian's Facility Management Handbook.* New York: Neal-Schuman.

Velleman, Ruth A. 1990. *Meeting the needs of people with disabilities: a guide for librarians, educators, and other service professionals.* Phoenix, AZ: Oryx Press.

Journal Articles and Published Papers

Eggett, Colleen B. 2002. Assistive technology needs in public libraries: A survey. *Journal of Visual Impairment & Blindness*, August, 549–57.

Flippo, Karen F., Katherine J. Inge, and J. Michael Barcus. 1995. *Assistive technology: a resource for school, work, and community.* Baltimore: P.H. Brookes Pub. Co.

National Council on Disability (U.S.). 2000. *Federal policy barriers to assistive technology.* Washington, DC (1331 F St., NW, Suite 1050, Washington 20004-1107): National Council on Disability.

Rubin, Rhea Joyce. 2001. *Planning for library services to people with disabilities.* ASCLA changing horizons series, #5. Chicago: Association of Specialized and Cooperative Library Agencies.

Rubin, Richard E. 2004. *Foundations of Library and Information Science.* New York. Neal-Schuman Publishers Inc.

Watchfire. *WebXM—Accessibility Testing.* Accessed November 24, 2007. Available at http://www.watchfire.com/products/webxm/bobby.aspx.

Case Law

U.S. Court of Appeal, 7th Circuit. 1988. *Anderson v. University of Wisconsin.* 841 F.2d 737, 740.

U.S. Court of Appeal, 11th Circuit. 1990. *United States v. Board of Trustees for the University of Alabama.* 908 F.2d 740.

U.S. Department of Education, Office of Civil Rights. 2007. *How to File a Discrimination Complaint with the Office for Civil Rights*. Accessed November 27, 2007. Available at http://www.ed.gov/about/offices/list/ocr/docs/howto.html.

U.S. Department of Education, Office of Civil Rights. 1991. *St. Charles County Community College (MI)*. 1 NDLR par. 348.

U.S. Department of Education, Office of Civil Rights. 1995. *Nova Southeastern University (FL)*. 7 NDLR par. 27.

U.S. Department of Education, Office of Civil Rights. 1995. *Patrick*. 7 NDLR par. 470.

U.S. Department of Health and Human Services. 2003. *The New Freedom Initiative*. Accessed November 19, 2007. Available at http://www.hhs.gov/newfreedom/init.html.

U.S. Department of Justice. 1993. *Title II Technical Assistance Manual* Section III-4.3600.

U.S. House. 2007. *College Opportunity and Affordability Act of 2007*. 110th Cong., first session, H.R. 4137. Accessed November 26, 2007. Available at http://thomas.loc.gov/cgi-bin/query/D?c110:1:./temp/~c110z98Cub::.

U.S. Senate. 2007. *Higher Education Amendments of 2007*. 110th Cong., first session, S. 1642. Accessed November 26, 2007. Available at http://thomas.loc.gov/cgi-bin/bdquery/z?d110:SN01642:@@@D&summ2=2&.

U.S. Supreme Court. 1979. *Southeastern Community College v. Davis*. 442 U.S. 397.

U.S. Supreme Court. 1985. *Alexander v. Choate*. 469 U.S. 287.

United States. 2001. *Library and information services for individuals with disabilities: an NCLIS hearing in Washington, DC, July 8, 1999*. Darby, PA: Diane Pub.

United States. 2002. *Assessing the Assistive Technology Act of 1998 hearing before the Subcommittee on 21st Century Competitiveness of the Committee on Education and the Workforce, House of Representatives, One Hundred Seventh Congress, second session, hearing held in Washington, DC, March 21, 2002*. Washington, DC: U.S. Government Printing Office.

United States and Educational Resources Information Center. 1998. *Auxiliary aids and services for postsecondary students with disabilities: higher education's obligations under Section 504 and Title II of the ADA*. Washington, DC: U.S. Department of Education, Office for Civil Rights.

Technology

Access Inc. n.d.. *The ADA Accessibility Stick II*. Retrieved January 9, 2009, from http://www.adastick.com.

Anson, D. 2002. College Misericordia, *Magic Slope Block*. U.S.A.

Necessary Measures. ADA Stick, *Necessary Measures, Inc.*, U.S.A.

Kim, J. B. and Brienza, D. M. 2006. Development of a remote accessibility assessment system through three-dimensional reconstruction technology. *Journal of Rehabilitation Research & Development*, 43(2), 257–272.

NOTES

1. Huprich, Julia and Green, Ravonne. "Assessing the Library Homepages of COPLAC Institutions for Section 508 Accessibility Errors: Who's Accessible, Who's

Not, and How the Online WebXACT Assessment Tool Can Help." *Journal of Access Services*. Binghampton, NY: Haworth Press, 6(1&2), 59–74.

2. Trotta, Carmine and Trotta, Marcia. *The Librarian's Facility Management Handbook*. New York: Neal-Schuman, 2001.

3. Association of Specialized and Cooperative Library Agencies. *Revised Standards and Guidelines of Service for the Library of Congress Network of Libraries for the Blind and Physically Handicapped*, Chicago: ALA, 2005.

4. American Library Association Committee for Accreditation Standards. *Standards for Accreditation of Master's Programs in Library & Information Studies, 2008* (http://www.pla.org/ala/educationcareers/education/accreditedprograms/standards/standards_2008.pdf).

5. Americans with Disabilities Act. 1990. *U.S.C.* Vol. 42, sec. 12101. Public Law 101-336 The Americans with Disabilities Act of 1990.

6. Ibid.

7. Ibid.

8. Rehabilitation Act, Section 504. 1973. *U.S. Code Annotated*. Vol. 29, sec. 794.

9. Americans with Disabilities Act. 1990. *U.S.C.* Vol. 42, sec. 12101. *Public Law 101-336 The Americans with Disabilities Act of 1990*.

10. Henderson, Cathy. "2001 College Freshmen with Disabilities: A Biennial Statistical Profile." Washington, DC: American Council on Education/HEATH Resource Center.

11. Green, Ravonne and Gillespie, Diane. "Assistive Technologies in Academic Libraries: A Preliminary Study," *Portal* 1(3), 329–338.

12. Americans with Disabilities Act. 1990. *U.S.C.* Vol. 42, sec. 12101. *Public Law 101-336 The Americans with Disabilities Act of 1990*.

13. Ingle, Emma, Green, Ravonne, and Huprich, Julia. "How Accessible Are Public Libraries' Web Sites? A Study of Georgia Public Libraries," *Journal of Access Services*. Binghampton, NY: Haworth Press, 6(1&2).

14. Trotta and Trotta. *The Librarian's Facility Management Handbook*.

15. Americans with Disabilities Act Accessibility Guidelines Checklist for Buildings and Facilities (http://www.access-board.gov/adaag/checklist/a16.html).

16. Ibid.

SECTION IV

Universal Access

CHAPTER 7

Universal Access: Promoting Better Library Services for All

We have discussed the various Microsoft accessibility applications in previous chapters. These applications are certainly helpful to individuals with disabilities but they are useful to many other individuals. These options can be activated from the control panel following the instructions provided in earlier chapters and through Microsoft.

Universal design has become increasingly important in our society. Our focus in designing new buildings, renovating existing spaces, and planning academic programs is more on utility and comfort than on aesthetics. This chapter provides an overview of the legal obligations for providing an accessible work and learning environment in postsecondary education, universal design principles for instruction, and specific tips and resources for helping some specific disability groups.

Green (1999) conducted a survey of Research I institution libraries to determine the type and level of support that these libraries offered individuals with disabilities.[1] Green's study found that only 30 percent of the libraries surveyed offered specific services and technologies for individuals with disabilities. This study followed a study conducted by Dr. Howard Kramer (1998) at the University of Colorado-Boulder indicating that only 12 percent of Research I institutions offered adequate assistive technology support for individuals with disabilities.[2] Both of these studies indicated that only a minimal number of libraries stated that they offered special services for individuals with disabilities on their web sites, had a designated librarian to coordinate accessibility services for individuals with disabilities, or provided assistive technologies.

Green (2008) replicated the Green (1999) of Research I institution libraries survey and found that all of these libraries except one now have a link from their library web sites with information regarding services for patrons with disabilities.[3] All of the libraries that have a web link have a coordinator for disability services. All of these libraries offer special services for individuals with disabilities, such as book retrieval, note taking, photocopy services, and accessible furnishings. All of these library web sites list information about contacting the campus disability services coordinator and connecting with services beyond the library. All of these libraries list a selection of assistive technology equipment that is readily available for individuals with visual and hearing disabilities. Most of these web sites state specific policies for providing services for individuals with disabilities. Two universities (University of Michigan-Ann Arbor and the University of California-Berkeley) specifically mention technologies and services that are available for individuals with learning disabilities.

The Green (1999) study was conducted to give an indication of the state of special library services in general.[4] This survey along with a follow-up Delphi study was quite useful for determining trends in library special services. The special services librarians at these institutions were good sources for soliciting expert opinion and for determining guidelines for improving services for patrons with disabilities.

The Green (2008) study indicates that libraries are generally working to adopt the spirit of the law and not just the minimal letter of the law, as was indicated in previous surveys.[5] This is an encouraging finding for all of us that seek to provide accessible services to all. However, there is still much work to do in providing information and appropriate training for librarians to adequately and appropriately serve the needs of individuals with disabilities.

The Tech Act provides an avenue for all individuals with disabilities to explore the use of AT. It is the responsibility of the individual in a library setting or in any other postsecondary educational setting to disclose his or her disability to the appropriate individual.[6] It is the individuals' responsibility to seek sources for funding for assistive technologies for personal use. Such funding is usually available for personal assistive technology devices through the Department of Vocational Rehabilitation Services. Individuals and institutions may obtain information and assistance through their states' assistive technology project. Types of information and assistance may include computer accessory devices and modifications of existing equipment.

When an individual discloses the need for adaptive equipment that would not be considered for personal use, it would be the responsibility of the institution to seek funding and to secure such equipment. Items such as optical scanning equipment, large-print keyboards and fonts, large monitors, enlarged text for automated card catalog systems and other library indices, microfiche or microfilm and touch screens, telecommunication devices, speech synthesizers and brailled materials would all be examples of items that the institution or library would be responsible for providing for patrons with disabilities.

The Carl D. Perkins Vocational and Applied Technology Education Act Amendments (1990) addresses the responsibility of postsecondary schools to provide aids and services for patrons with disabilities equal to those of their non-disabled peers.[7]

Principles of universal design become increasingly important as librarians add information literacy courses and other instructional modules. Access issues in higher education are defined as design issues in the inclusive classroom environment. This allows for the spectrum of multiple intelligences and learning modalities and the broad diversity that contemporary learners and teachers bring to the classroom, live or delivered through distance education.

The Association of College and Research Libraries (ACRL) states that the role of instruction and information literacy continues to grow in the academic library. Librarians are faced with a need to develop a more focused set of skills based on utilizing universal design principles to teach effectively. The ACRL "Information Literacy Competency Standards for Higher Education," the ACRL Information Section's "Guidelines for Instruction Programs in Academic Libraries," and the "Standards for Proficiencies for Instruction Librarians and Coordinators" should be a basis for broader library discussions regarding the skills necessary to create library instruction and information literacy programs.[8] One of the deficiencies indicated by this group was the need for librarians who were proficient in the area of instructional design.

Universal design when applied to higher education goes beyond accessible design for people with disabilities to make all aspects of the educational experience more inclusive for all involved in the course by building in consideration of a great variety of characteristics, including those related to gender, race/ethnicity, age, stature, disability, and learning style.[9]

Most libraries have as their mission to provide accessible services and materials for everyone. The Internet, Web 2.0, and falling technology prices should make universal accessibility a reality.

Text-to-speech software and other technologies have been around for quite a while and the production costs should be minimal. Professionals should be aware of adaptive technologies and services and funding and training should be available for adaptive technologies. While universal access should be the norm, in reality it is not.

We have examined many technologies that are available for individuals with disabilities. Many of these technologies are fairly inexpensive but may still be out of reach with library budgets that are already strained. Educational and institutional license fees and other hidden expenses make the costs more prohibitive.

Even technologies that are free require a staff person's time to install the software, to master using the software, and to train other staff members and patrons to use the software. The staff members in most libraries are already overextended in many cases and do not have time for extra duties.

Many libraries have one or a small number of specific workstations for individuals with disabilities. It is certainly better to have something rather than nothing. However, many individuals with disabilities strongly dislike being singled out as different or special. Individuals without disabilities sometimes need to use the special workstations for foreign language studies, technical material, enlarging print, or other uses. They cannot schedule the use of this equipment because it is in such short supply and high demand by individuals with disabilities. Clearly, universal access is the ideal in any library setting.

Some professionals believe that this singled-out factor negatively affects the pricing on assistive technology products. A singled-out software line for persons with disabilities creates a market where the price elasticity of demand is very low. Despite the price of assistive technologies, the quantity of demand for assistive products is likely to remain stable because there are no viable alternatives. Suppliers have no incentive to reduce their prices.[10]

Government grants are available for assistive technology, and some would argue that adding money to the accessibility software pie further increases the demand for the product. Additional funding may in fact only increase the price of the software even more. Grants increase the gap between the have's and the have not's. Some libraries that receive grant funding have the necessary technologies to support accessible services and others do not. Here are some things that libraries can do to counteract the accessibility dilemma:

- Use Microsoft Accessibility Options and other free ware.
- Consider open source alternatives—For instance Ubuntu offers a screen reader as part of the package. If you have a Ubuntu station, you are offering an assistive technology station without calling it that Ubuntu still needs improvements but libraries should utilize this software and provide feedback to Linux.
- AIMS offers a product that will read DAISY format on a Windows platform.
- Partner with community groups to insist that all OEM software includes a viable and easy-to-use accessibility system, including a one-click screen resizer and a screen reader.
- Make existing accessibility stations seem the same as other stations.
- Fulfill your obligations for free access, but do not forget about the big picture. We need to start innovating ways to serve patrons with visual impairments if we truly want to maintain our reputation of offering "Access for All."
- Purchase only products that are universally accessible as much as possible. The more we consider accessibility a "special" add-in, the more the costs of "specialness" get born on those with disabilities.[11]

Deines-Jones (2007) recommends several services for individuals with disabilities that are free or low cost to make the library more safe and user-friendly for everyone. Signs should be clear, aisles should be clean, and reference points should be clearly identified. All doors particularly in main traffic areas should not require more than five pounds of force. Heavy doors are difficult for individuals with mobility problems to maneuver. Heavy doors are difficult for anyone with a large stack of materials to manage. Senior citizens and children may have difficulty with heavy doors.[12]

Uneven flooring, single steps, or difficult transitions provide a barrier for individuals in wheel chairs and individuals with vision problems. However, flooring problems may be hazardous to anyone and should be corrected. Clutter such as stacks of books or journals should not block movement in any public areas. Deines-Jones (2007) recommends a daily walk through the library to make sure that all walkways are clear of obstructions.[13] Keeping walkways clear and clean makes a safer environment for everyone. Some of the main things to check daily are that floors are dry and clear of any obstacles or debris. Check to make sure that the entrance mat edges are flat. Hazardous areas and wet floors should be marked. Check to make sure that signage is clear and accurate. Signs and banners should not be low enough to hit tall patrons with visual impairments in any public access areas. Check to make sure that displays, plants, and furnishings do not block access in any area. Check light fixtures throughout the library and at the entrance to make sure that they are working and contact maintenance personnel if bulbs need to be replaced or if fixtures are not operational.

VISUAL AND HEARING

Making your library more accessible to individuals with visual and hearing impairments in many cases makes the library environment more appealing and accessible to everyone. Proper lighting is crucial for individuals with visual impairments. Proper lighting is important for individuals with hearing impairments when they are trying to read lips.[14] Good lighting helps to provide a safer, more inviting environment for everyone.

Signs should be clear and bold with adequate contrast. Make sure that signs are not blocked by any large objects. Use large, bold letters. Avoid using script, calligraphy, and other stylistic fonts. Some of the following color contrast schemes work best for individuals with visual impairments. Bright yellow background with black lettering, bright blue background with white or yellow lettering, and black background with white lettering are all usually good choices. Handouts should be provided or at least available in large print. Library maps and diagrams should be available in large print and should clearly indicate emergency exits, accessible restroom facilities, areas that may not be accessible, and service points. Braille signs should be placed consistently at the standard height in elevators and throughout the library. Ask individuals with visual impairments what format they need or prefer and if they have color preferences for background and print on handouts.

Test public announcement systems, emergency alarms, and alarms for individuals with disabilities on a regular basis. Make sure that the volume is sufficient in various parts of the building and that the sound is clear. Periodically test any alarms for individuals with disabilities with these individuals to make sure that they are functioning properly.

Providing a welcoming atmosphere for everyone will ensure that individuals with disabilities feel welcome as well. Most principles of good etiquette for patrons in general are good etiquette for individuals with disabilities. Here are a few things that help to provide a welcoming atmosphere for everyone:

Greet all patrons and make eye contact with them as you greet them. Merchants have long recognized the importance of greeting customers and making eye contact as soon as they enter your store or department. Customers or library patrons are much more likely to feel comfortable with asking for assistance if someone has acknowledged them and has shown them a welcoming attitude. If a patron has an interpreter or comes with a caregiver, speak directly to the patron and not to the interpreter or caregiver. In order to make direct eye contact with the patron, you might need to sit down if they are in a wheel chair or if they are shorter than you are. If you sit at a desk, try to place a chair beside your desk instead of in front of your desk so that your desk does not appear to be a barrier.

Do not use condescending language when speaking to children, senior citizens, or those with disabilities. Do not use such terms as *dear* when talking with individuals with special needs. Such terms give the impression that you consider the patron to be mentally incompetent. Do not touch a person with a disability unless he or she asks you to assist him or her physically in some way.

Service animals accompany individuals with various disabilities. Most of us have seen service dogs that accompany blind people. Now there are service animals that accompany people with many different disabilities. Individuals with seizure disorders may have an assistive pet to alert them to an impending seizure. Individuals with some mobility problems have an assistive pet to retrieve objects for them. It is best to assume that a pet might be an assistive pet when a person enters the library with a pet. You might politely ask about the pet when the person enters the building just to confirm that fact and then inform other library staff about the pet so that the patron will not have to answer repeated questions about the service animal. Another possibility would be to place a sign at the door or on the web site indicating that assistive pets are welcome to visit the library with their owners and to request that the owners inform someone at the circulation desk about their pet.

Do not shout or exaggerate your speech in any way when you are assisting individuals with hearing impairments. You might write down your responses if the person continues to have difficulty hearing you. If the person uses sign language and you do not, try to find a staff member that knows sign language. A staff training in basic sign language is good. Teaching staff to sign so that they can at least give directions to the restrooms, the reference desk, and other main points is a good start.

High shelving will be inaccessible for individuals in wheel chairs. Climbing step stools may not be advisable for small children, senior citizens, or individuals with visual impairments. Individuals that have suffered back or knee injuries may have difficulty bending over to reach items on lower shelves. Try to anticipate special needs and accompany individuals with special needs to the stacks when they request materials or send someone with them. However, if shelving is low and it should not be a problem to retrieve materials, the individual may wish to function independently. You might offer to provide a small, low cart or basket for them to retrieve items.

LEARNING STYLES AND LEARNING DIFFERENCES

We are constantly dealing with people with different learning styles and in some cases individuals with learning disabilities. Some people prefer to process information graphically and have excellent map reading skills. Other people have difficulty with maps and need written directions. If someone asks for directional assistance, you might ask whether they would prefer a map or written text. Have both formats available and ask if they need to have either the map or the text enlarged.

Information overload is a temptation for any information science professional. Try to determine exactly what the patron needs and provide him or her with the information that he or she is requesting. Superfluous details and information beyond the individual's needs waste time and can be confusing to the patrons. If a fifth grader is doing a paper on global warming, do not suggest graduate level professional society papers on the topic. Be clear and concise in providing instructions. Consider learning styles. If the patron is showing signs of boredom or disinterest, ask follow-up questions to make sure that you are meeting his or her needs. Walk with the patron to the stacks if you think that he or she might have difficulty locating or retrieving material.

CONCLUSIONS

An environment that is free of clutter, provides clear signage, and has barrier-free walkways is welcoming to everyone. Providing training and materials for staff to address various learning styles and special needs immediately makes individuals with special needs and all patrons to feel welcome.

RESOURCES

Journal Articles

Creamer, Debbie. "Universal Instructional Design for Libraries." *Colorado Libraries*, 2007, Vol. 33, Issue 4, pp. 12–15.

Epp, Mary Anne. "Closing the 95% Gap: Library Resource Sharing for People with Print Disabilities." *Library Trends*, Winter 2006, Vol. 54, Issue 3, pp. 411–429.

Felix, Lisa. "Design for Everyone." *Library Journal*, 10/1/2008, Vol. 133, Issue 16, pp. 38–40.

Mates, Barbara. "Rethinking Resource Sharing: Universal Design." *Interface*, Spring 2008. Vol. 30, Issue 1, pp. 1–2.

Neumann, Heidi. "What Teacher Librarians Should Know about Universal Design." *Teacher Librarian*, December 2003, Vol. 31, Issue 2, pp. 17–20.

Riley, Cordelia. "Training for Library Patrons Who Are Hard of Hearing." *Journal of Access Services*, 2009, Vol. 6, Issue 1/2, pp. 72–97.

Web Site

University of North Carolina Center for Universal Design—http://www.design.ncsu.edu/cud/

Dictionaries and Encyclopedias

Dictionary of Disability Terminology (PDF)/edited by David Blocksidge. Singapore: Disabled People's Association (www.dpa.org.sg/Publications/download.asp?download1=dictionary).

The Fairchild Dictionary of Interior Design/Martin M. Pegler; with illustrations by Ron Carboni. 2nd ed. New York: Fairchild, 2006.

Design Guides and Handbooks

For web-based dictionaries and encyclopedias go to Electronic Resources link on your library's homepage.

Accessible Design Review Guide: An ADAAG Guide for Designing and Specifying Spaces, Buildings, and Sites/the Accessible Space Team, Robert Grist. [et al.]. New York: McGraw-Hill, 1996.

The Accessibility Checklist: An Evaluation System for Buildings and Outdoor Settings. Berkeley, CA: MIG Communications, 1992.

Americans with Disabilities Act Accessibility Guidelines: A Checklist for Buildings and Facilities. Los Angeles: BNi Building News, 1996.

Barrier Free Design Handbook—published by the Veterans Administration. Office of Facilities Management (http://www.va.gov/facmgt/standard/access_overview.asp).

CalDAG 2003: *California Disabled Accessibility Guidebook: Interpretive Manual & Checklist for the Design, Construction and Inspection of Public*

Accommodations, Commercial Buildings, Publicly Funded Housing and Transportation Facilities/Michael P. Gibbens. 5th ed., millennia. Canoga Park, CA: Builder's Book, Inc., 2003.

Disability Access Symbols, by *The Graphic Artists Guild*. Twelve symbols used to promote and publicize accessibility of places, programs, and activities for people with various disabilities (http://www.gag.org/resources/das.php).

Handbook on Standards and Guidelines in Ergonomics and Human Factors/edited by Waldemar Karwowski. Mahwah, N.J.: Lawrence Erlbaum Associates, 2006. Human Factors and Ergonomics.

Pocket Guide to the ADA: Americans with Disabilities Act Accessibility Guidelines for Buildings and Facilities/Evan Terry Associates. Rev. ed. New York: John Wiley & Sons, 1997.

Time Saver Standards for Housing and Residential Development/edited by Joseph De Chiara, Julius Panero, Martin Zelnik. 2nd ed. New York: McGraw-Hill, 1995.

Time Saver Standards for Interior Design and Space Planning/[edited by] Joseph De Chiara, Julius Panero, Martin Zelnik. New York: McGraw-Hill, 2001.

Time Saver Standards for Urban Design/editors, Donald Watson editor-in-chief, Alan Plattus, Robert G. Shibley. 1st ed. New York: McGraw-Hill, 2003.

Universal Design Handbook/Wolfgang F.E. Preiser, editor in chief; Elaine Ostroff, senior editor; foreword by Robert Ivy. New York: McGraw-Hill, 2001.

Article Indices

Architecture—indexes and abstracts—*use for articles on design, projects, and practice.*

Regulatory Resources

The Access Board—Accessibility Laws (http://www.access-board.gov/about/laws/).

Accessible and usable buildings and facilities/secretariat, International Code Council; approved February 13, 1998, American National Standards Institute. Falls Church, VA: The Council, c1998. ICC/ANSI A117.1—Accessible and Usable Buildings and Facilities (index only) (http://www.iccsafe.org).

ADA Home—Department of Justice (http://www.ada.gov/).

ADA Standards for Accessible Design—U.S. Department of Justice (http://www.ada.gov/stdspdf.htm).

ADA: *Americans with Disabilities Act Architectural Barrier Removal & Compliance Manual: A Simplified Approach to Accessibility.* 4th ed. Granada Hills, Calif.: James E. Jordan; Anaheim, Calif.: Distributor to the trade, BNi Building News, c1994. Based on Supplement to the California Building Code (part 2, Title 24 C.C.R.) Effective April 1, 1994, and Uniform Federal Accessibility Standards.

ADAAG—Accessibility Guidelines for Buildings and Facilities (http://www.access-board.gov/adaag/).

Americans with Disabilities Act and Architectural Barriers Act Accessibility Guidelines/United States Access Board. Architectural and Transportation Barriers Compliance Board. Washington, D.C.: United States Access Board [2004] issued online. Codes: Guides and Manuals.

Design for Barrier-Free, Accessible, and Universal Design

Accessible Housing by Design: Universal Design Principles in Practice/Steven Winter Associates. New York: McGraw-Hill, 1997.

Accessible Housing: Quality, Disability and Design/Robert Imrie. England, New York: Routledge, 2006.

The Assist Guidebook to the Accessible Home: Practical Designs for Home Modifications and New Construction/prepared by Salt Lake City, Utah: Assist, Inc., 2002.

Barrier Free Design: A Manual for Building Designers and Managers/James Holmes-Siedle. Oxford: Butterworth Architecture, 1996.

Beautiful Universal Design: A Visual Guide/Cynthia A. Leibrock, James Evan Terry. New York: John Wiley, 1999.

A Blueprint for Action: A Resource for Promoting Home Modifications/compiled by the Center for Universal Design. Raleigh, NC: The Center, 1997 (http://www.usc.edu/go/hmap).

Consumer's Guide to Home Adaptation/ed. Tom Noll; ill., Linda Bourke. Boston, MA: Adaptive Environments Center, 2002 printing.

Countering Design Exclusion: An Introduction to Inclusive Design/Simeon Keates and John Clarkson. London; New York: Springer, 2003.

Design for Independent Living: The Environment and Physically Disabled People/by Raymond Lifchez and Barbara Winslow. New York: Whitney Library of Design, 1979.

Gracious Spaces: Universal Interiors by Design/Irma Laufer Dobkin and Mary Jo Peterson. NY: McGraw-Hill, 1999.

High-Access Home: Design and Decoration for Barrier-Free Living/Charles A. Riley, II. New York: Rizzoli, c1999.

Inclusive Design: Design for the Whole Population/edited by John Clarkson. [et al.]. London; New York: Springer, c2003. 608 p.: ill. ; 25 cm. EnvDesign TA174. I464 2003.

Inclusive Design: Designing and Developing Accessible Environments/Rob Imrie and Peter Hall. London; New York: Spon Press, 2001.

Readily Achievable Checklist: A Survey for Accessibility/project director, Elaine Ostroff; authors: James Gary Cronburg, Joshua Barnett, and Nancy Goldman. Updated and rev. ed. Boston, MA: Adaptive Environments Center, 1993, 1991.

Universal and Accessible Design for Products, Services, and Processes/Robert F. Erlandson. Boca Raton: CRC Press, 2008.

Universal Design: A Manual of Practical Guidance for Architects/Selwyn Goldsmith with PRP Architects; CAD drawings by Jeanette Dezart. Oxford; Boston: Architectural Press, 2000.

Universal Design: Creative Solutions for ADA Compliance/Roberta L. Null with Kenneth F. Cherry. Belmont, Calif.: Professional Publications, 1996.

The Universal Design File: Designing for People of All Ages and Abilities/authors, Molly Follette Story, James. Rev. ed. North Carolina: NC State University, Center for Universal Design, 1998.

Universal Design—Division of the State Architect (DSA) (http://www.dsa.dgs.ca.gov/UniversalDesign/default.htm).

Human Dimension/Ergonomics

*Environmental Ergonomics: The Ergonomics of Human Comfort, Health, and Performance in the Thermal Environment.*1st ed. Amsterdam; Boston: Elsevier, 2005. Elsevier ergonomics se; v.3.

Human Dimension and Interior Space: A Source Book of Design Reference Standards/by Julius Panero and Martin Zelnik. New York: Whitney Library of Design, 1979.

Human Factors Methods: A Practical Guide for Engineering and Design/Neville A. Stanton. [et al.]. Aldershot, England; Burlington, VT: Ashgate Pub. Co., 2005.

International Encyclopedia of the Social & Behavioral Sciences (IESBS) UCB Only. *The Measure of Man and Woman: Human Factors in Design*/Alvin R. Tilley; Henry Dreyfuss Associates; Rev. ed. New York: Wiley, c2002, in Engineering. *Methods in Environmental and Behavioral Research*/edited by Robert B. Bechtel, Robert W. Marans, and William Michelson. New York: Van Nostrand, 1987.

Public Places and Private Spaces: The Psychology of Work, Play, and Living Environments/Albert Mehrabian. New York: Basic Books, 1976.

Design for Community

The Access Manual: Auditing and Managing Inclusive Built Environments/Ann Sawyer and Keith Bright. Oxford; Ames, Iowa: Blackwell, 2004.

Designing for the Homeless: Architecture That Works/Sam Davis. Berkeley: University of California Press, 2004.

Humanistic Design of Assisted Living/John P. Marsden. Baltimore: Johns Hopkins University Press, 2005.

Inclusive Urban Design: Streets for Life/Elizabeth Burton and Lynne Mitchell. Oxford; Burlington, MA: Architectural Press, 2006.

Planning & Designing the Physically Active Community. Resource List/American Planning Association, May 2003 (http://www.planning.org/research/active/).

Transitional Housing: A Bridge to Stability and Self-Sufficiency: Best Practices in Program Design and Delivery. San Francisco, CA: Homebase, Center for Common Concerns, 1998.

Links

- ADA Publications—U.S. Department of Justice (http://www.ada.gov/publicat.htm)
- Adaptive Environments Inc.—http://www.adaptiveenvironments.org/
- Designing for the 21st Century: An International Conference on Universal Design (http://www.designfor21st.org)
- Home Modifications Organization—http://www.homemods.org/
- AIA—American Institute of Architects (http://www.aia.org/)
- ASID—American Society of Interior Designers (http://www.asid.org/)
- BOMA—Building Owners and Managers Association International (http://www.boma.org)

- Center for Universal Design—http://www.design.ncsu.edu/cud/
- DisabilityInfo.gov—http://www.disabilityinfo.gov
- ICC—International Code Council (http://www.iccsafe.org/)
- National Council on Disability—http://www.ncd.gov/
- Creating Livable Communities
- NIBS—National Institute of Building Sciences (http://www.nibs.org/)
- United States Access Board (http://www.access-board.gov)

NOTES

1. Green, Ravonne. *Virginia Polytechnic Institute and State University Benchmarking Institutions and Library Services for Individuals with Disabilities Survey.* 1999. Unpublished survey.

2. Kramer, Howard. *Research I Institutions and Assistive Technology Availability for Individuals with Disabilities.* 1998. Unpublished survey.

3. Green, Ravonne. "Research I Institutions and Library Services for Individuals with Disabilities Survey." 2008. Unpublished survey.

4. Green, 1999.

5. Green, 2008.

6. Assistive Technology Act. 2004. *U.S.C.* Vol. 29, sec. 3001.

7. The Carl D. Perkins Vocational and Applied Technology Education Act Amendment of 1990, 20 U.S.C. § 301 et seq.

8. Association of College and Research Libraries. Guidelines for Instruction Programs in Academic Libraries. Chicago: American Library Association. 2003.

9. Passman, Tina and Green, Ravonne. "Start with the Syllabus: Universal Design from the Top." *Journal of Access Services*, 6(1&2), 48–47.

10. Deschamps, Ryan. "Will Universal Accessibility at Libraries even be Possible in Ten Years?" *The Other Librarian*, Oct. 25, 2007 (http://otherlibrarian.wordpress.com/2007/10/25/will-universal-accessibility-at-libraries-even-be-possible-in-10-years/).

11. Deschamps, 2007.

12. Deines-Jones, Courtney. "Low-cost/No-cost Ways to Improve Service Right Now," in *Improving Library Services to People with Disabilities*. Ed. By Courtney Deines-Jones. Chandos: London, 2007.

13. Ibid.

14. Ibid.

SECTION V
Staff Training

CHAPTER 8

Library Disability Training

The main purposes of a library disability training program should be to eliminate unlawful discrimination, to promote equality of opportunity for individuals with disabilities, and to develop policies and best practices to best serve the needs of individuals with disabilities.

Developing a training plan to serve individuals with disabilities is much like developing any other aspect of library training. The top priority should be involving individuals with disabilities throughout the planning and implementation processes. We will discuss forming a committee in the next chapter. Scherer (2006) stated that the main reason why many assistive technology devices were not used is because consumers were not involved in their selection and were not trained to use these devices.[1]

One of the mandates of the ADA (Title III) is that libraries should solicit public comment regarding the self-evaluation plan for serving individuals with disabilities. Cooperative relationships will be a necessity in order to provide the best quality services and materials for patrons.[2] A transition team for accessibility should be appointed that includes a wide representation of all areas of responsibility. Individuals with disabilities should be appointed to this ad hoc committee. Some individuals do not need to attend all committee meetings.

The transition team will recommend and encourage the best use of resources to meet the information needs of library staff and patrons with disabilities. One of the first tasks of the group should be to carry out an access audit. The ADA checklist that is offered in Chapter 6 is an example of a facility audit. The International Federation of Library Associations (IFLA) checklist compiled by Irvall and Nielsen (2005) is an excellent plan for auditing the library facility as well as materials and equipment for individuals with specific disabilities. The transition team should make specific recommendations to help improve both the physical space in the libraries and general services to staff and patrons.

Disability training like any other training plan includes the analysis, planning, implementation, and control of carefully formulated programs designated to bring about voluntary exchanges of values with target goals for the purpose of achieving organizational objectives.

STAFF AWARENESS

Even though it may be advantageous in some respects to assign one staff member with the responsibility for special services, it is imperative that the library staff take a team approach to special services. One of the most disturbing problems nationwide with regard to library services and individuals with disabilities is the lack of knowledge and sensitivity on the part of library staff.

All libraries need to provide training to increase empathy for individuals with disabilities and awareness of the needs of individuals with various disabilities. The Roads to Learning program available from the American Library Association is an excellent training tool for this purpose. There are fact sheets available on each disability on the National Dissemination Center for Children with Disabilities (NICHCY) web site that are helpful for increasing staff awareness of a particular disability. There are numerous information sheets available at the Council for Exceptional Children web site. Training should take place on a regular and an ongoing basis as questions and needs arise. An initial general disabilities training workshop will help to provide basic information and to address empathy issues.

Some of the functions of a good training program include attitudes, relevant government legislation, commonly used adaptive technology, and communication strategies. The program should be evaluated on a regular basis and changed and updated as necessary. Input should be encouraged from staff members regarding training needs and approaches.

The program should provide a basic level of knowledge to enable staff to conduct reference interviews with individuals with disabilities. Some of the specific areas of staff development would include assisting staff in the development of appropriate communication skills, dispelling misconceptions and negative attitudes toward individuals with disabilities, providing staff with necessary collection development skills, and assisting staff in the assessment of current and future accommodations and facilities.

TRAINING METHODS

Several different training methods may be used. The team should consider the advantages and disadvantages of each. One method is not necessarily preferable. Some methods work better in certain settings and some methods are a better fit for certain learning styles. The ideal is to provide trainings in several different formats to accommodate as many individuals as possible. Some of the different methods might include the following:

- One or more face-to-face workshops on various disabilities and disability issues
- One or more online workshops on various disabilities and disability issues
- A face-to-face training provided by an external trainer
- A repository of online resources on disability issues
- A web-based course using the university's web courseware

DEVELOPING THE MODULE

A sub-group of the transition team may consist of librarians, disability professionals, an IT or AT technician, and at least one faculty member with web development experience. *The ADDIE Instructional Design Model*, available at http://www.intulogy.com/addie/, is an excellent model for designing either a face-to-face or a web-based training. The ADDIE model first presents an *analysis* of training needs. The analysis is used to drive course *design* and *development*. The training module is *implemented* first as a pilot version, and an *evaluation* of the learning materials is conducted with the pilot group that will be used to improve the course.[3]

The learning outcomes should be clearly stated in the course introduction. The IFLA report recommends including the following themes in the training: "legislation, the language of disability, inclusive practices for employees and patrons, using assistive technology to support people with disabilities, and using and creating materials in alternative formats."[4]

The design of the course should be consistent. For example, each unit or module should include lecture notes and readings, activities, discussion topics, and additional resources on the topic.

Lecture notes and readings should provide concise, substantive materials on common disabilities. The activities should encourage interaction either in person or on a discussion board or wiki in a web-based environment. Participants might discuss their commute to work and how this would have been different if they would have had a particular disability.

An assessment piece should always be available to obtain feedback for improving training. At the end of the course, questionnaires, a post-study quiz, and projects such as pathfinders on disability resources and topics, web blogs, and web pages help to assess the effectiveness of the module. End-of-course projects provide materials for future iterations of the course.

LIBRARIES WITH DISABILITY RESOURCES
FOR TRAINING PROGRAMS

Public

Brooklyn Public Library—http://www.brooklynpubliclibrary.org/internet_links
_detail.jsp?linklistpageid=1122
Missouri Department of Mental Health—http://www.dmh.missouri.gov/mrdd/
libservices/library.htm
Monroe County Library—http://www.libraryweb.org/buildingbridge.html
Springfield Library—http://www.springfieldlibrary.org/liblinks/disabil.html

Academic

New Jersey State Library—http://www.njstatelib.org/LDB/Disabilities/dsresrcs.php
University of Wisconsin-River Falls Chalmer Davie Library—http://www.spring
fieldlibrary.org/liblinks/disabil.html
West Virginia State University—http://evac.icdi.wvu.edu/library/training.htm

Other

Earnworks—http://www.earnworks.com/docs/FactSheets/Employer/FS-ER-Diversity
SenstivityTraining.pdf
United States Department of Labor—http://www.dol.gov/dol/topic/training/
disabilitytraining.htm
University of Wisconsin Family Village—http://www.familyvillage.wisc.edu/
General/Disability-awareness.html
Virginia Department of Rehabilitative Services—http://www.vdrs.org/downloads/
TrainingPkt.pdf

Etiquette

City of Sacramento—http://www.cityofsacramento.org/adaweb/learning_about
_disabilities.htm
Community Resources for People with Disabilities—http://www.crinet.org/
etiquette.php
Easter Seals—http://www.easterseals.com/site/PageServer?pagename=ntl_etiquette
Job Accommodation Network—http://www.google.com/search?hl=en&rlz=1T4
ADBF_enUS287US287&q=disability+etiquette&revid=1394953134&ei=mib
2SZrNHIeqtgeYvOm3Dw&sa=X&oi=revisions_inline&resnum=0&ct=broad
-revision&cd=7
Memphis Center for Independent Living—http://www.mcil.org/mcil/mcil/etiqu01.htm
United Spinal Association—http://www.unitedspinal.org/pdf/DisabilityEtiquette.pdf
University of Northern Iowa—http://www.uni.edu/equity/DisabilityEtiquette.shtml

Bibliography

Abledata—http://www.abledata.com.
Agada, J. and Dauenheimer, "Beyond ADA: Crossing Borders to Understand the
Psychosocial Needs of Students with Disabilities," in H.A. Thomson (ed.)

Crossing the Divide: Proceedings of the Tenth National Conference of the Association of College and Research Libraries. Chicago: ALA: 295–302.

Charles, Sandra and Foster, Moria. 2004. *Supporting Library Users with Disabilities: A Guide for Front-line Staff.* 2nd ed. Dundee: University of Dundee. (http://scurl.ac.uk/WG/SNG/documents/DisabilityBooklet1.5version2no%20 pics.doc) (accessed April 11, 2009).

Delin, A. 2003. *Audits* (http://www.mla.gov.uk/documents/dis_guide04.pdf) (accessed April 11, 2009).

Disability Rights Commission, 2003. *Good Practice Guide—Libraries and Learning Centres* (http://www.drcgb.org/publicationsandreports/publicationhtml.asp? id=203&docsect=0&section=ed) (accessed April 11, 2009).

Forrest, Margaret E.S. 2006. "Towards and Accessible Academic Library: Using the IFLA Checklist." *IFLA Journal*, 32, no. 1: 13–18, available at http://www .ifla.org/V/iflaj/IFLA-Journal-1-2006.pdf (accessed July 18, 1008).

Forrest, Margaret E.S. 2007. "Disability Awareness Training for Library Staff: Evaluating an Online Module." *Library Review*, 56, no. 8: 707–715.

Forrest, Margaret E.S. August 2008. *E-learning to Support the Development of Disability Awareness Skills: A Case Study.* Edinburgh, United Kingdom: IFLA Meeting: 80. Libraries Serving Disadvantaged Persons (http://www.ifla.org/ IV/ifla74/index.htm) (accessed April 11, 2009).

Hernon, Peter and Calvert, P. (eds.) *Improving the Quality of Library Services for Students with Disabilities.* Westport, CN: Libraries Unlimited, 2006.

INTULOGY (2006), *The ADDIE Instructional Design Model*, available at http:// www.intulogy.com/addie/ (accessed April 11, 2009).

Irvall, Bergitta and Nielsen, Gyda. 2005. *Access to Libraries for Persons with Disabilities: Checklist.* The Hague: International Federation of Library Associations. IFLA Report # 89 (http://www.ifla.org/VII/s9/nd1/iflapr-89e.pdf) (accessed April 11, 2009).

TRAINING RESOURCES

Attitudes/Communication/Etiquette

American Library Association (ALA) Roads to Learning.

Deines-Jones, Courtney. "Low-cost/No-cost Ways to Improve Service Right Now" in *Improving Library Services to People with Disabilities*. Ed. By Courtney Deines-Jones. Chandos: London, 2007.

Deines-Jones, Courtney and Van Fleet, Connie. *Preparing Staff to Serve Patrons with Disabilities.* Neal-Schuman: New York, 1995.

Specific Disabilities

Council for Exceptional Children (CEC).

Deafness video series—http://sfpl.lib.ca.us/librarylocations/accessservices/ deafservices.htm.

National Dissemination Center for Children with Disabilities (NICHCY).

Organizations

American Library Association: Association of Specialized and Cooperative Library Agencies (http://www.ala.org/ala/ascla/ascla.htm).

International Foundation of Library Associations: Libraries Serving Disadvantaged Persons Section http://www.ifla.org VII/s9/index.html.

The National Service for the Blind and Physically Handicapped (http://www.loc.gov/nls).

World Federation of the Deaf (http://www.wfdeaf.org).

Americans with Disabilities Act Training

International Foundation for Library Associations (IFLA) IFLA Checklist.

Assistive Technology

Rochester Institute of Technology (http://library.rit.edu).

Microsoft Vendors

These vendors provide hardware and software that are compatible with Microsoft. These partners have a proven track record of designing, building, and supporting assistive technology products that help individuals with difficulties and impairments to successfully use computers. Many of these vendors offer 30-day trials and training.

- AbleLink Technologies, Inc.
- Academic Software, Inc.
- Acapela
- ACE Centre
- AD Information & Communications Co., Ltd.
- Adobe Systems, Inc.
- Ai Squared
- AnthroTronix
- Applied Human Factors
- Assistive Technology, Inc.
- Aurora Systems Inc.
- Baum
- BayFirst Solutions LLC
- Benetech
- Biolink Computer R&D Ltd.
- Blink Twice, LLC
- Brain Actuated Technologies, Inc.
- Brain Logic
- CameraMouse, Inc.

- CAST
- Claro Software
- Code Factory, S.L.
- Compusult Limited
- Compuware Corp.
- Crick Software Inc.
- Cyberkinetics Neurotechnology Systems, Inc.
- DAIR Computer Systems
- Dancing Dots Braille Music Technology, L.P.
- DataHand Systems, Inc.
- DEAFWORKS
- Deque Systems Inc.
- Design Science
- Designer Appliances Inc.
- Dolphin Computer Access
- Don Johnston Incorporated
- Duxbury Systems, Inc.
- DynaVox Systems LLC
- EITAC Solutions Group, LLC
- Enabling Technologies
- E-Ramp Inc.
- EyeTech Digital Systems
- Freedom Scientific
- FrogPad, Inc.
- Gennum Corp.
- gh, LLC
- Gus Communications Inc.
- GW Micro
- H. K. Eyecan Ltd.
- Handy Tech Elektronik GmbH
- HIMS Co., Ltd.
- HiSoftware
- HumanWare
- IBM
- IGEL Kompaniet AS
- In Touch Systems
- Infogrip, Inc.
- Innovation Management Group, Inc.
- IntelliTools, Inc.
- Keybowl, Inc.
- Kurzweil Educational Systems, Inc.
- Laureate Learning Systems Inc.
- LC Technologies, Inc.

- Madentec
- Mayer-Johnson, Inc.
- McFarland Technology, Inc.
- Metroplex Voice Computing, Inc.
- NaturalPoint Inc.
- Nuance
- NXi Communications, Inc.
- Optelec
- Origin Instruments
- Polital Enterprises LLC
- Portset Systems Ltd.
- PPRDirect
- Premier Assistive Technology
- Quantum Technology Pty Ltd
- Realize Software Corp.
- RehabTool LLC
- Remedy Interactive
- RJ Cooper & Associates, Inc.
- Ryobi Systems Solutions
- Science Accessibility Net
- Serotek Corp.
- Somatic Digital
- SVOX AG
- TACK-TILES Braille Systems LLC
- Talking Communities
- TASH, Inc.
- Technology For Education, Inc.
- Techno-Vision Systems Ltd.

NOTES

1. Scherer, Marcia. J. *Institute for Matching Person & Technology, Inc.* (2006). Retrieved January 9, 2009, from http://members.aol.com/IMPT97/MPT.html.

2. Americans with Disabilities Act. 1990. *U.S.C.* Vol. 42, sec. 12101. Public Law 101-336 The Americans with Disabilities Act of 1990.

3. INTULOGY. (2006). *The ADDIE Instructional Design Model*, available at http://www.intulogy.com/addie/ (accessed April 11, 2009).

4. Kavenaugh, R., and Skold, B.C. *Libraries for the Blind in the Information Age: Guidelines for Development*, IFLA Professional Reports No. 86, International Federation of Library Associations and Institutions, 2005. available at http://www.ifla.org/VII/s31/pub/Profrep86.pdf.

SECTION VI

Assistive Technology and Disability Services Marketing

CHAPTER 9

Marketing Tips for Serving Individuals with Disabilities

Deines-Jones (2007) describes some of the barriers to library use for individuals with disabilities. Some of the barriers that she indicates include the following: assuming there is nothing "for us" in the library because they believe that the library offers only traditional print materials; identifying the library as a government institution causes individuals with disabilities to mistrust libraries because they have in many cases not received the support and services that they have needed from government agencies; believing that librarians will not be able to communicate with someone with their particular disability (i.e., sign language or other special communication needs); and negative past experiences.[1]

Marketing outreach services to the disability community may include both disability-specific and general community organizations of which many individuals with disabilities may participate. These may include non-government organizations, senior citizens' groups, advocacy groups, schools, faith-based organizations, and other community groups.[2]

Developing a marketing plan to serve individuals with disabilities is much like developing any other aspect of library marketing. The top priority should be to involve individuals with disabilities throughout the planning and implementation processes.

Marketing services for individuals with disabilities, like any other marketing plan, include the analysis, planning, implementation, and control of programs designated to bring about voluntary exchanges of values with target markets in order to achieve organizational objectives. The marketing plan relies heavily on designing the organization's services in terms of the target market's needs, desires, communication, and services to inform and motivate those services.[3]

Weingand (1999) emphasizes seven major points in Kotler's definition.

1. Marketing is a *managerial* process involving analysis, planning, implementation, and control.
2. Marketing is concerned with *carefully formulated programs*—not random actions—designed to achieve desired responses.
3. Marketing seeks to bring about *voluntary exchanges*.
4. Marketing selects *target markets* and does not seek to be all things to all people.
5. Marketing is directly correlated to the achievement of *organizational objectives*.
6. Marketing places emphasis on the target market's preferences (consumer's needs and *desires* rather than on the producer's preferences).
7. Marketing utilizes what has been termed the *marketing mix* or the 6 Ps: *product, pricing, place*/distribution, *promotion*/communication, the marketing audit (*prelude*) and evaluation (*postlude*) (p. 4).[4]

Walters (2004) identified two more P's: positioning and politics.
The first "P," *prelude* or the marketing audit, has three facets:

1. Evaluating the library environment. The facilities should be evaluated in terms of ADA compliance, available technologies, and services for individuals with disabilities. Considering the library environment within the context of the community or college environment would be important too.
2. Evaluating the mission, goals, objectives, and programs of the library within the context of disability services.
3. Evaluating current library marketing activities within the context of disability services.

Products are typically considered as output measures or tangible items. Products for individuals with disabilities might include specific equipment, furnishings, alternative format materials, specific services such as individualized reference or circulation services, programs, and instruction products. Walters (2004) recommends asking questions about the purpose, needs, costs, and benefits related to each product that is identified.

Price or budget for accomplishing the mission, goals, objectives, and programs of the library for serving individuals with disabilities is a prime consideration. Direct costs as well as indirect costs should be considered in planning and evaluating the benefits of services.

Place is not necessarily a physical location. The online catalog and many electronic books, journals, and reference databases are available remotely now. Libraries must consider accessibility issues with all resources for all patrons. The physical facility is still an important factor in developing and managing the library marketing plan for individuals with disabilities. ADA guidelines should be consulted as a part of developing the marketing plan.

Promotion is a strong key in any successful marketing effort. The library will want to adequately inform potential patrons with disabilities about the materials, equipment, and services that are available at the library. Additionally, the library can promote volunteering to serve in various capacities such as note taking, reading, book retrieval, photocopying, signing, and other services.

Positioning involves the community or college perception of your library or service. A library can be well positioned as an effective conduit of service to individuals with disabilities if it follows the spirit of the law and not just the letter. Libraries should maintain good working relationships with all campus and community offices that coordinate disability services, administrators, faculty, and students with special needs. Additionally, forming good relationships with donors and funding agencies is important.

Politics is an important part of any marketing plan. Politics and positioning are closely aligned in any organization. Forming close ties and keeping good communication lines open with administrators about the budget and ongoing planning is essential to any effective marketing effort. Showing specific value-added services and outcomes is one of the most significant ways to politic for additional funding.

Postlude or evaluation plans demonstrate the overall effectiveness of any marketing plan. Formative and summative evaluations can be conducted throughout the planning process to ensure effective planning efforts.[5]

DEVELOPING AN ACTION PLAN

Developing an action plan for physical accessibility will involve issues such as cost, whether your building can accommodate physical changes, and current accessibility issues with your building such as physical access, lighting, alarms, and signage.

Seven Areas of Planning for an Inclusive Model for Patrons with Disabilities

There are seven primary areas of library planning: facilities, equipment, materials, services, training, funding, and cooperative relationships. The library has traditionally been the center of learning on college campuses. The educational, research, and public service programs of the institution should include equal opportunities for all learners.

These seven key planning areas were selected because they are most often cited as needs in the literature on library policies and services for individuals with disabilities. These seven areas are consistent with good overall library planning. The intent is to provide a consistent, practical model for library planning and services for patrons with disabilities. This is an inclusive approach. Services should be included throughout the general library program. Such efforts involve cooperative planning on the part of the entire library staff, faculty representatives, and individuals with disabilities, community volunteers, and field experts. A libraries' plan for disability services should involve cooperative relationships in order to provide the best quality of materials and services and to secure the necessary funding for these resources. It is important to involve a representative group of individuals in order to promote awareness and to facilitate positive attitudes toward persons with disabilities.

Facility Planning

The physical accessibility of the library facility is the most important concern. The previous chapter on facilities describes physical accessibility requirements under the Americans with Disabilities Act of 1990.

Materials

Providing equal access to all library materials for all patrons may not be possible initially but it should be the ultimate goal. Many materials are now available in alternate formats for individuals with disabilities. Closed caption media, for example, are available for most classic titles and do not cost any more than media that do not contain this feature. Most standard reference books and many classic novels for literature, history books, and religious texts and current periodicals are available on audiocassette from the Library of Congress: Library for the Blind and Handicapped. Many textbooks and other materials are available from regional the Library for the Blind and Dyslexic centers. Low-vocabulary books for students who have learning disabilities or other reading disabilities are available from local public libraries. Regional Talking Book Centers have collections of recreational or general informational reading materials for all age levels. They can request other materials from the Library for the Blind and Handicapped. Items from the Library for the Blind and Handicapped are sent directly to the patrons' home. There are no postage charges for returning these items.

Many software programs for individuals with disabilities are free or in the public domain. One of the best sources for software for persons with disabilities is the Gallaudet Software-to-Go program. This service supplies thousands of software programs at no cost to libraries that serve individuals with disabilities. The library pays an annual subscription fee and may borrow any of the materials listed in the Software-to-Go catalog. Titles are available in every subject area and grade level and for a wide range of disabilities.

Most assistive technology companies offer demonstration disks. These demonstration disks can be helpful to librarians in the selection process. It is often difficult to determine if software will be appropriate to the needs of the user without having the opportunity to use it. This is particularly important with expensive reference software or software that is being purchased for the needs of one individual.

Reputable vendors will supply a satisfied customer list for specialized software. This is helpful to make initial contacts with other libraries that have used a particular software package to learn about bugs and glitches and to have a local support group for exchanging ideas for potential software uses.

Some of the same sources listed for reviewing adaptive equipment review assistive software. Some professional journals now have a section on materials for inclusion or software for special needs. It is important to evaluate assistive technology using the same quality collection development standards as would be used for the remainder of the library collection.

The collection development policy should include a statement about deselecting assistive materials as they become dated using parameters similar to the rest of the collection. Deselection policies are particularly important with reference works.

We have discussed disability training in general in the last chapter. Most assistive software will not require special training. However, some more specialized software may require special workshops for staff. All staff should be encouraged to participate in such training. It is important to keep staff informed of any upgrades or changes to adaptive equipment. Refresher courses are good to ensure that everyone's skills are current. It is always important to ask the vendor if special training will be provided and the costs involved with such training. Most assistive technology vendors provide training at no cost. Some provide web sites with computer-based training.

Training manuals, toll-free help numbers, and web addresses should be maintained with the software if they are not available within the software.

Services

A library can compensate for the lack of the most up-to-date equipment at least somewhat by providing additional services. Services should be publicized on the library web site, in the library literature, and in library signage. A sign should be posted on the front door or at the main circulation desk inviting patrons with disabilities to request assistance. It is particularly important that patrons with learning disabilities and other hidden disabilities disclose their disabilities to library staff in order to receive proper assistance.

Some of the services that are typically most necessary include book finding and photocopying. A person in a wheel chair cannot reach books or periodicals that are over the 42-inch reach range. Individuals with dyslexia may need assistance with locating books on the shelves. Individuals with fine motor difficulties may need assistance. Students who have visual or motor difficulties may need assistance with photocopying services. The zoom feature on the copier can be used to enlarge materials that are not available in large print. Materials copied from the microfiche reader/printer can be copied and enlarged on the photocopier.

Most academic libraries recognize the need for identifying an individual who is responsible for special services or an ADA coordinator. Sometimes patrons will not feel comfortable with disclosing their disabilities to someone at a public reference desk but will feel comfortable with going to someone's office that is identified as a special services person and talking with that individual about their disability and their special library needs privately.

Special services for individuals with disabilities as well as any special procedures or forms for obtaining these services should be indicated on the library web site. Contact information of individuals who may assist with special services should be included on the library web site.

Funding

The library should make an effort to request reference software and other general books and materials with adaptive options. Vendors often do not mention adaptive options or may not be aware of them. Any training for new software should include adaptive features. The library should encourage each department to request materials for individuals with special needs in their individual disciplines. If there is a developmental studies program, this area should have an allocation to provide materials for English as a second language and other specialized needs. This allocation may be used for the purchase of books, software, or media or for costs incurred with borrowing materials.

Some assistive devices and equipment are covered under individual health insurance plans. The primary funding need in most libraries is to provide a basic collection of assistive equipment and Windows-based software. Some institutional funds should be allocated for this purpose on an annual basis. There are a number of outside sources such as Tools for Life that provides information about available funding for assistive technology. The Tools for Life publication, *Dollars and Sense*, is a helpful funding resource.

It will be important to provide funds for maintenance and upgrades of equipment and software and for training. Additional funding for publications in alternate formats and for signs and disability information brochures will be necessary. Any budgets for furnishings and building additions or alterations will need to include funds for accommodations for persons with disabilities.

Cooperative Relationships

As noted in the previous chapter, one of the mandates of the ADA (Title III) is that libraries should solicit public comment regarding the self-evaluation plan for serving individuals with disabilities.[6]

Cooperative relationships will be a necessity in order to provide the best quality services and materials for patrons. A Transition Team for Accessibility should be appointed that includes a wide representation of all areas of responsibility. Individuals with disabilities should be appointed to this ad hoc committee. Some of these individuals may not need to attend all committee meetings. The physical plant person, for example, would only need to come to meetings when building alterations or additions are included on the agenda. Other field experts and vendors may be included as necessary. Ideally, meetings should occur at least twice a year. One of the main purposes of these meetings should be to address student concerns. A suggestion box or an electronic counterpart should be available for patrons with disabilities to express their needs and concerns regarding library services.

The transition committee should provide current information about disability issues and needs. They will play a vital role in recommending facility changes, materials, services, and training opportunities for individuals with disabilities. The transition team will help to inform the library staff and other members about funding opportunities.

After the transition committee has completed its initial assessments of the status of the library in filling its mission to individuals with disabilities, this committee may not need to meet on a regular basis. The library should revisit the plan that this committee has developed and should continue to appoint individuals with disabilities as well as individuals with expertise in the areas of disabilities and assistive technologies to serve on the library committee.

Marketing Tips

The library disability services link or web page should include the following information:

Facilities

- Campus accessibility maps
- Facilities accommodations (restrooms, drinking fountains, parking, elevator locations, carrels with wheelchair access)
- Conference and meeting room access
- Emergency exits and emergency plans for individuals with disabilities
- Telephone and TTD service

Accessing Library Materials

- Photocopier and microfilm services
- Book and other retrieval services
- Interlibrary loan services
- Home delivery

- Online public catalog assistance
- Remote access to electronic databases
- Volunteer services such as readers, note takers, or sign language interpreters)

Library Instruction and Special Training

- Guides for equipment and services
- Tutorials for equipment

Circulation and Reference Services

- Ask-A-Librarian Link
- Individual Research Consultation
- Borrowing and Return Procedures and Policies

Assistive Technology

- Assistive technology equipment that is available and any special training or requirements for using this equipment

Communication

- Link to library home page
- Contact information for the designated librarian(s) responsible for disability services
- Links to other campus or community disability services agencies
- Library service guidelines or policies regarding documentation and eligibility requirements for special services
- Information about volunteer opportunities (library committee, special committee for assistive technology or disabilities, note takers, readers, sign language, and other opportunities)
- Link to request special services

Alternative Collections

- Large print
- Braille
- Talking Books
- E-textbooks and reserves
- Ebooks

RESOURCES

Books and Papers

Bates, Mary Ellen. *Free, Fee-Based and Value-Added Information Services*. Ed. Donna Anderson. Factivia (April 2002) (http://ww.factiva.com/collateral/files/whitepaper_feevsfree_032002.pdf).

Cutlip, Scott and Allen H. Center. *Effective Public Relations*. Englewood Cliffs, NJ: Prentice-Hall, 1994.

Deines-Jones, Courtney. *Improving Library Services to People with Disabilities*. London: Chandos, 2007.

Fisher, Patricia and Pride, Marseille. *Blueprint for Your Library Marketing Plan: A Guide to Help You Survive and Thrive*. Chicago: ALA, 2005.

Kotler, Philip. *Marketing for Nonprofit Organizations*, 2nd ed. Englewood Cliffs, NJ: Prentice-Hall, 1982.

Lindsay, Anita. *Marketing and Public Relations Practices in College Libraries*. Chicago: ALA: College Libraries Section of the Association of College and Research Libraries, 2005.

Reed, Sally Gardener, Nawalinski, Beth, and Peterson, Alex. *101+ Great Marketing and Fundraising Ideas for Libraries and Friends*. New York: Neal-Schuman, 2004.

Ross, Catherine and Dewdney, Patricia. *Communicating Professionally*, 2nd ed. NY: Neal-Schuman Publishers, 1998.

Siess, Judith A. *The Visible Librarian: Asserting Your Value with Marketing and Advocacy*. Chicago: ALA, 2003.

Walters, Suzanne. *Library Marketing That Works!* NY: Neal-Schuman Publishers, 2004.

Weingand, Darlene. *Customer Service Excellence: A Concise Guide for Librarians*. Chicago: ALA, 1997.

Weingand, Darlene. *Future-Driven Library Marketing*. Chicago, ALA, 1999.

Wolfe, Lisa. *Library Public Relations, Promotions, and Communications*, 2nd ed. NY: Neal-Schuman Publishers, 2005. This book has a lot of information about building your library's brand, planning, and evaluation.

Woodward, Jeannette. *Creating the Customer-Driven Library: Building on the Bookstore Model*. Chicago: ALA, 2005.

Journals

Alcock, Jo. "Using Facebook Pages to Reach Users: The Experiences of Wolverhampton." *ALISS Quarterly*, January 2009, Vol. 4, Issue 2, 2–6.

Barry, Peggy L. "Top Ten Communication Tips for Communication and Outreach." *ILA Reporter*, February 2009, Vol. 27, Issue 1, 8.

Cleve, Marigold and Stephens Derek. "National Library Web Sites: How Do They Market the Library." *Alexandria*, 2008, Vol. 20, Issue 2, 67–79.

Cram, Laura. The Marketing Audit: Baseline for Action. *Library Trends*, 1995, Vol. 43, 326–349.

Datson, Emma. "Selling Libraries." *Australian Library Journal*, November 2008, Vol. 57, Issue 4, 453–454.

Enache, Ionel. "The Theoretical Fundamentals of Library Marketing." *Philobiblon*, 2008, Vol. 13, 477–490.

Ford, Vikki. *PR*: "The State of Public Relations in Academic Libraries." *College and Research Libraries*, 1985, Vol. 46, 395–401.

Information Today. MLS Marketing Library Services. (June 2002). Information Today. Available at http://www.infotoday.com/mls/mls.htm (accessed March 19, 2004).

Jarvis, Margo. "Anatomy of a Marketing Campaign." *Computers in Libraries*, September 1998, Vol. 18, 64–78.

Johnson, K.M. "Wonder Woman: Marketing Secrets for the Trillion Dollar Customer." *Choice: Current Reviews for Academic Libraries*, January 2009, Vol. 46, Issue 5, 956.

Kassel, Amelia. "Marketing: Realistic Tips for Planning and Implementation in Special Libraries; Market the Importance of Librarians, the Caretakers of Libraries Adapt to the Ever-Changing Forms of Knowledge." *Information Outlook*, 2006, Vol. 6, 6–10.

Keller, James A. "Branding and Marketing Your Library." *Public Libraries*, September/ October 2008, Vol. 47, Issue 5, 45–51.

Kelly, Brian, Sloan, David, Brown, Stephen, Seale, Jane, Lauke, Patrick, Ball, Simon, and Smith, Stuart. "Accessibility 2.0: Next Steps for Web Accessibility." *Journal of Access Services*, 2009, Vol. 6, Issue 1/2, 265–294.

Kemp, Jane and Laura Witschi. *Displays and Exhibits in College Libraries*. CLIP Notes #25. Chicago: ACRL/ALA, 1997.

Kendall, Sandra and Susan Massarella. "Prescription for Successful Marketing." *Computers in Libraries*, 2001, Vol. 21, 28–34.

King, Helen. "Stop! Here!" *The Australian Library Journal*, 2003, Vol. 52, 90–92.

Morgan, Eric Lease. "Marketing Future Libraries." *Computers in Libraries*, 2001, Vol. 18, 28–34.

Morrison, Ian. "Library Management and Marketing in a Multicultural World." *Australian Academic & Research Libraries*, September 2008, Vol. 39, Issue 3, 218.

OCLC. "Marketing May Hike Library Funding." *American Libraries*, August 2008, Vol. 39, Issue 7, 29.

Orphan, Stephanie. "ACRL Marketing Efforts Expand." *American Libraries*, 2003, Vol. 34, 10–12.

Saas. Rivkah K. "Marketing the Worth of Your Library." *Library Journal*, 2002, Vol. 127, 37–38.

Smykla, Evelyn Oritz. "SPEC Kit: Marketing and Public Relations in ARL Libraries." SPEC Kit. 240; Summary. Association of Research Libraries, April 1999. Available at http://www.sla.org/chapter/cwcn/wwest/v1n3/cavilb 13.htm.

Special Libraries Association. "Public Relations, Marketing, Advocacy." Special Libraries Association. Available at http://www.sla.org/chapter/cwcn/wwest/ v1n3/cavilb13.htm.

Wilson, Charlotte and Roger Strouse. "Marketing Tips for Information Professionals." February 1, 2002.

Library Marketing Web Sites

ACRL Marketing Web Site—http://www.ala.org/ala/acrl/acrlissues/marketingy
ourlib/marketingyour.cfm

ALA Marketing Public Libraries—http://www.pla.org/ala/pla/committeework/
marketingpublic.cfm

ALA PRTalk News listserv—listproc@ala.org

@your library campaign—http://www.librarysupportstaff.com/marketinglibs.html

Elsevier Marketing for Libraries—http://www.elsevier.com/framework_librarians/
LibraryConnect/LCP08/LCP08.pdf

Gale Market Your Library—http://gale.cengage.com/free_resources/marketing/
index.htm

Library Marketing Blog—http://librarymarketing.blogspot.com/

Mahady, Tara. *Creating Community Through Your Communications Campaign
Associations.* http://campagn.com/community_print.html (accessed March 19,
2009).

Marketing Corporate Libraries—http://www.insitepro.com/donald3.htm

Marketing Public Libraries—http://www.olc.org/marketing/instructions.htm

MLS Marketing Library services—http://www.infotoday.com/MLS/default.shtml

The "m" word blog—http://themwordblog.blogspot.com/

MODEL LIBRARY WEB SITES WITH DISABILITY SERVICES LINKS

Academic Libraries

Arizona State University—http://lib.asu.edu/ada

Boston University (has an extensive list of etext libraries and alternative music resources)—http://www.bu.edu/disability/resources/alternative.html

Brooklyn College Library—http://dewey.brooklyn.cuny.edu/resources/service.jsp
?sub_id=69

Clemson University—http://www.lib.clemson.edu/libservices/access.htm

College of William and Mary—http://swem.wm.edu/services/disabilityservices.cfm

Columbia University—http://www.columbia.edu/cu/lweb/services/lio/disability.html

Cornell University—http://wwwbeta.library.cornell.edu/svcs/disability

El Centro College—http://www.elcentrocollege.edu/Student_Services/Disability/

Harvard University—http://www.extension.harvard.edu/2008-09/resources/
disability.jsp

Lane Community College Library—http://www.lanecc.edu/library/services/ds/
disability.htm

Louisiana State University—http://www.lib.lsu.edu/ref/adaptive.html

New York University Libraries—http://library.nyu.edu/services/disabilities.html

North Carolina Agricultural and State University—http://www.library.ncat.edu/
services/Disability%20Services%20Brochure08.pdf

North Carolina State University—http://www.lib.ncsu.edu/accessibility/resources/

North Dakota State University—http://www.library.nd.gov/DisabilityServices.html

Ohio State University—http://library.osu.edu/sites/libinfo/disability.php

Oklahoma State University—http://www.library.okstate.edu/services/disabil.htm

Oregon State University—http://osulibrary.oregonstate.edu/research/guides/
      perdis.htm
Philadelphia University—http://www.philau.edu/disabilityservices/libraryservices.htm
San Jose State University Libraries—http://www.sjlibrary.org/services/disability/
      paging.htm
Smith College—http://www.smith.edu/library/services/disability/
Southern Adventist University—http://library.southern.edu/cms/services/information/
      disability
Southern Illinois University-Carbondale—http://www.lib.siu.edu/resources/hand
      outs/DisabilitySupportServices.pdf
Spoon River College—http://www.src.edu/disability-services
Syracuse University—http://library.syr.edu/research/Internet/education/disability
      studies.html
Texas A & M—http://www.src.edu/disability-services
Texas State University—http://www.library.txstate.edu/services/accessibility.html
University at Albany-SUNY (this site contains an excellent guide and an online
      disability registration form for services)—http://dev.library.albany.edu/spwd/
University of Central Florida Libraries (this site has some excellent links to W3C
      information)—http://library.ucf.edu/Services/DisabilityServices.asp
University of Colorado-Boulder—http://ucblibraries.colorado.edu/about/disabilities.htm
University of Georgia—http://www.libs.uga.edu/disabil/disabilities.html
University of Hawaii-Kapiolani—http://kapiolani.hawaii.edu/page/disability
University of Illinois at Chicago—http://www.uic.edu/depts/lib/services/disabilities/
University of Kentucky—http://www.uky.edu/Libraries/page.php?lweb_id=13
University of Michigan—http://www.lib.umich.edu/hsl/about/specialneeds.html
University of Michigan Health Sciences Library—http://dewey.brooklyn.cuny.edu/
      resources/service.jsp?sub_id=69
University of Minnesota—http://www.lib.umn.edu/site/disserv.phtml
University of Mississippi—http://www.olemiss.edu/depts/general_library/files/ref/
      accessibility.html
University of Missouri-Kansas City—http://library.umkc.edu/disability
University of Montana-Helena College of Technology—http://www.umhelena.edu/
      CurrentStudents/DisabilityServices/tabid/283/Default.aspx
University of North Carolina—http://www.lib.unc.edu/brauer/disability.html\
University of North Carolina-Greensboro—http://library.uncg.edu/depts/circ/
      disabledServices.asp
University of North Carolina-Wilmington—http://library.uncw.edu/web/outreach/
      disabilities.html
University of Northern Colorado—http://library.unco.edu/services/disability
      services.htm
University of Oregon—http://libweb.uoregon.edu/general/services/disability
      services.html
University of South Carolina Library—http://www.sc.edu/library/disservices.html
University of Texas at San Antonio—http://lib.utsa.edu/Services/General/Disabilities/
University of Utah—http://disability.utah.edu/marriottlibrary.html
University of Wisconsin-Madison Libraries—http://memorial.library.wisc.edu/ser
      vices/disability.html

University of Wisconsin-River Falls (this site contains an accommodation request form)—http://www.uwrf.edu/library/info/policies/disabilityservices.php

West Virginia State University—http://www.libraries.wvu.edu/disability/

Public Libraries

Alameda County Library—http://www.aclibrary.org/services/adaServices/default.asp?topic=ADAServices&cat=ADAServices

Berkeley Public Library—http://www.berkeleypubliclibrary.org/services_and_resources/disability_resources.php

Mansfield Public Library—http://www.sailsinc.org/mansfield/html/disability_services.html

Mobile Public Library—http://www.mplonline.org/service.htm

Oakland Public Library—http://www.oaklandlibrary.org/disabilityservices.html

Pima County Public Library—http://www.library.uni.edu/pubpol/dispolpub.pdf

Plymouth Public Library—http://www.plymouthpubliclibrary.org/disabilityservices.htm

San Diego Public Library—http://www.sandiego.gov/public-library/services/disability.shtml

Monroe County Public Library—http://www.monroe.lib.in.us/general_info/disabilityserv.html

Other Resources

Centre for Disability Studies—http://www.leeds.ac.uk/disability-studies

CODI: Cornucopia of Disability Information—http://www.itcompany.com/inforetriever/dis-gen/htm

Disability Info.gov—http://www.disabilityinfo.gov

Disability Statistics Center supported by National Institute on Disability and Rehabilitation Research—http://www.dsc.ucsf.edu/main.php

Disability Studies and Links to Other Disability Resources—http://www.soeweb.syr.edu/thechp/disres.htm#studies

Disability Studies: Guide to Library Research—http://www.ryerson.ca/library/subjects/disability/print.html

Facilitated Communication Institute—http://www.soeweb.syr.edu/thef.ci

National Center for the Dissemination of Disability Research—http://www.ncddr.org

National Communication Association Disability Caucus—http://www.towson.edu/~bhalle/ncadis.html

National Institute on Disability and Rehabilitation Research (NIDRR)—http://www.ed.gov/about/offices/list/osers/nidrr/index.html

Office of Special Education and Rehabilitative Services (OSERS)—http://www.ed.gov/about/offices/list/osers/index.html

Women with Disabilities: Health and Aging—http://www.tigger.uic.edu/~lisab/homepage.htm

Oregon Ability—http://www.oregonability.org

Society for Disability Studies—http://www.uic.edu/orgs/sds
TASH: The Association for Persons with Severe Handicaps—http://www.tash.org
Wrightslaw: Special education law and advocacy for children with disabilities—
    http://www.wrightslaw.com
World Institute on Disability—http://www.wid.org
Yahoo! Disability Studies link—http://www.dir.yahoo.com/Social_Science/Disability
    _Studies

NOTES

    1. Deines-Jones, Courtney. "Low-Cost/No-Cost Ways to Improve Service Right
Now," in *Improving Library Services to People with Disabilities*. Ed. By Courtney
Deines-Jones. Chandos: London, 2007.
    2. Ibid.
    3. Kotler, Philip. *Marketing for Nonprofit Organizations*, 2nd ed. Englewood Cliffs,
NJ: Prentice-Hall, 1982.
    4. Weingand, Darlene. *Future-Driven Library Marketing*. Chicago, ALA, 1999.
    5. Walters, Suzanne. *Library Marketing That Works!* NY: Neal-Schuman Publishers,
2004.
    6. Americans with Disabilities Act. 1990. *U.S.C.* Vol. 42, sec. 12101. Public Law
101-336 The Americans with Disabilities Act of 1990.

INDEX

About the Authors

RAVONNE A. GREEN, PhD, is the author of *Library Management: A Case Study Approach*.

VERA BLAIR, MLIS, is a civil air patrol pilot who has conducted several assistive technology workshops for public libraries.